The official Raspberry Pi Camera Module guide, 2nd Edition

The official Raspberry Pi Camera Module guide, 2nd Edition
by David Plowman
ISBN: 978-1-916868-10-6
Copyright © 2024 Raspberry Pi, Ltd.
Printed in the United Kingdom
Published by Raspberry Pi, Ltd., 194 Science Park, Cambridge, CB4 0AB

Editor: Lucy Hattersley
Contributors: Nate Contino, PJ Evans, Phil King
Interior Designer: Sara Parodi
Production: Nellie McKesson, Brian Jepson
Photographer: Brian O'Halloran
Illustrator: Sam Alder
Graphics Editor: Natalie Turner
Publishing Director: Brian Jepson
Head of Design: Jack Willis
CEO: Eben Upton

November 2024: Second Edition
May 2020: First Edition

The publisher, and contributors accept no responsibility in respect of any omissions or errors relating to goods, products or services referred to or advertised in this book. Except where otherwise noted, the content of this book is licensed under a Creative Commons Attribution-NonCommercial-ShareAlike 3.0 Unported (CC BY-NC-SA 3.0).

Table of Contents

v   **Welcome**
vii   **About the author**

Chapter 1
1   Getting started
Learn about the different Raspberry Pi Camera modules and their capabilities

Chapter 2
17   More on still image capture
Resolutions, encoders, and file types

Chapter 3
27   More on Video Capture
Learn how to adjust video settings

Chapter 4
39   Preview Windows
Get to know the different types of preview windows

Chapter 5
47   Controlling the Camera
Learn how to adjust your camera settings

Chapter 6
59   Understanding Camera Modes
Choosing different camera modes

Chapter 7
67   Get started with Raspberry Pi AI Kit
Add neural processing to your camera

Chapter 8
77   Time-lapse photography
Make a device to capture photographs at regular intervals, then turn these images into a video

Chapter 9
83 High-speed photography
Make dazzling slow-motion clips of exciting events

Chapter 10
89 Use Python with Picamera2
Control your camera with code

Chapter 11
93 Stop-motion and selfies
Wire up a physical push-button to take photos

Chapter 12
101 Flash photography using an LED
Add an LED flash to shoot images in low light

Chapter 13
107 Make a spy camera
Set up a motion-activated spy camera in your room

Chapter 14
113 Smart door
Add a Raspberry Pi to your door with magical results

Chapter 15
123 Build a wildlife camera trap
Uncover the goings-on in your garden

Chapter 16
131 Take your camera underwater
Explore the underwater world with your camera

Chapter 17
141 Install a bird box camera
Observe nesting birds without disturbing them

Chapter 18
151 Live-stream video and stills
Stream video and regular stills to a remote computer

Welcome

Attaching a Camera Module to Raspberry Pi is a powerful way to expand its capabilities. With an image sensor attached, Raspberry Pi can capture high quality still images and record full HD video.

Raspberry Pi Camera Modules are easy to attach to your computer with a ribbon cable. This book walks you through all the different types of Camera Module, and how to attach them to Raspberry Pi and integrate vision technology to your projects.

The powerful *rpicam* apps and PiCamera2 Python library enable you to integrate Raspberry Pi Camera Module with your code. With the AI Kit attached to Raspberry Pi you can perform image recognition and other AI computing tasks.

In this book, you will discover how to attach a Camera Module to your Raspberry Pi, install the software, and code your own solutions. Our example projects explain how to perform image recognition, build time-lapse projects, wildlife camera traps, and live-stream video.

You can find example code and other information about this book, including errata, in its GitHub repository (**magpi.cc/camguidegit**). If you've found what you believe is a mistake or error in the book, or if you find something that could use clarification, please let us know by using our errata submission form at **magpi.cc/camguidefeedback**.

About the author

David Plowman is an engineer at Raspberry Pi with a special interest in camera software and algorithms, and image-processing hardware.

Colophon

Raspberry Pi is an affordable way to do something useful, or to do something fun.

Democratising technology — providing access to tools — has been our motivation since the Raspberry Pi project began. By driving down the cost of general-purpose computing to below $5, we've opened up the ability for anybody to use computers in projects that used to require prohibitive amounts of capital. Today, with barriers to entry being removed, we see Raspberry Pi computers being used everywhere from interactive museum exhibits and schools to national postal sorting offices and government call centres. Kitchen table businesses all over the world have been able to scale and find success in a way that just wasn't possible in a world where integrating technology meant spending large sums on laptops and PCs.

Raspberry Pi removes the high entry cost to computing for people across all demographics: while children can benefit from a computing education that previously wasn't open to them, many adults have also historically been priced out of using computers for enterprise, entertainment, and creativity. Raspberry Pi eliminates those barriers.

Raspberry Pi Press

store.rpipress.cc

Raspberry Pi Press is your essential bookshelf for computing, gaming, and hands-on making. We are the publishing imprint of Raspberry Pi Ltd, part of the Raspberry Pi Foundation. From building a PC to building a cabinet, discover your passion, learn new skills, and make awesome stuff with our extensive range of books and magazines.

The MagPi

magpi.raspberrypi.com

The MagPi is the official Raspberry Pi magazine. Written for the Raspberry Pi community, it is packed with Raspberry Pi-themed projects, computing and electronics tutorials, how-to guides, and the latest community news and events.

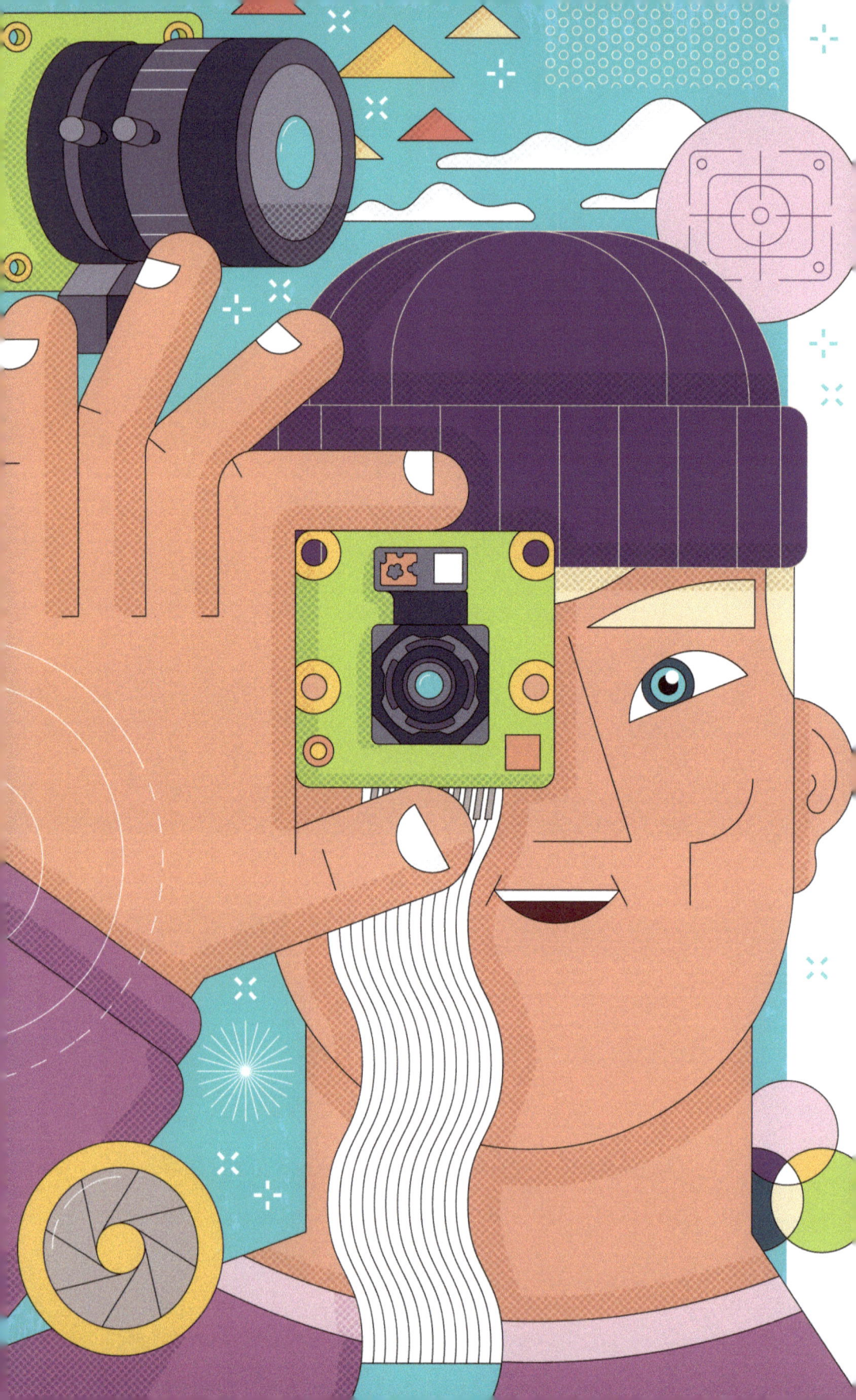

Chapter 1

Getting started

Learn about the different Raspberry Pi Camera modules and their capabilities

In this chapter, we'll introduce you to the range of different Raspberry Pi cameras and talk you through the particular features and benefits of each one. We'll show you how to connect them to Raspberry Pi and test that it is working correctly. Finally, we'll finish with a couple of simple examples that show you how to capture your first photo or video.

Getting to know your Raspberry Pi camera

Raspberry Pi has made five different types of cameras, of which all but the original v1 camera is currently in production. Some of them come in two or more different variants. Compatible camera modules are also made by a number of third-party suppliers, though we can't cover all of those in this book and — for any questions of support issues related to them — you might have to go back to the supplier where you bought the camera.

The official Raspberry Pi camera modules are:

- Raspberry Pi Camera Module
- Raspberry Pi Camera Module 2
- Raspberry Pi High Quality Camera
- Raspberry Pi Camera Module 3
- Raspberry Pi Global Shutter Camera

> More recently, Raspberry Pi has released the new AI Camera, which will be covered in subsequent revisions of this book.

Raspberry Pi Camera Module

Raspberry Pi's first official camera (**Figure 1-1**) was launched in 2013 and production ceased in 2017, because the sensor on which the camera is based is no longer available. However, a number of third-party sellers continue to sell v1 or v1-compatible cameras, and all Raspberry Pi camera software continues to support it.

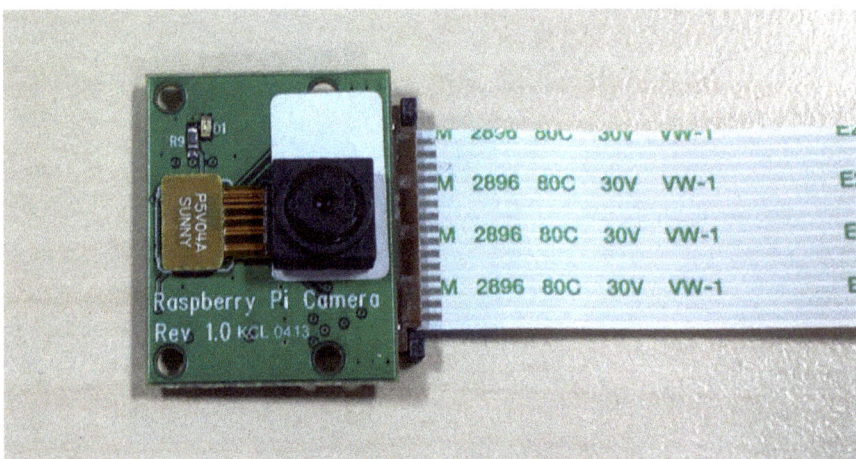

Figure 1-1 The original camera module

The camera is a 5MP device in a fixed focus module, with a maximum resolution of 2592×1944 pixels, and uses the Omnivision OV5647 image sensor. At lower resolutions, it is capable of up to 60 frames per second. It is suitable for still image photography and video recording.

Versions of this camera with the IR (infrared) filter removed have been available for specialised use cases.

Raspberry Pi Camera Module 2

Raspberry Pi Camera Module 2 (**Figure 1-2**) was introduced in 2018 to replace the original camera module and it comes in a similar small form factor. It offers broadly similar features and slightly improved performance.

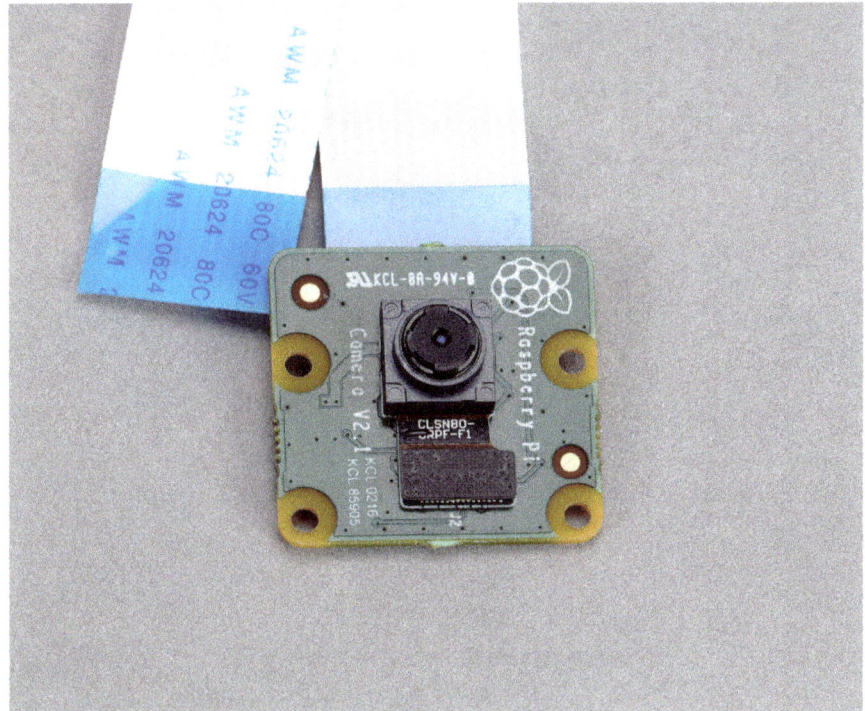

Figure 1-2   Camera Module 2

Camera Module 2 is an 8MP pixel device capable of outputting images at a maximum resolution of 3280×2464 pixels. It is capable of up to 100 frames per second at a VGA resolution and is based on Sony's IMX219 image sensor.

Like the original camera, it uses a fixed-focus lens though in this case you can adjust it manually using a tool supplied with the camera. This lets you increase the range of applications for which it can be deployed.

> **NoIR**
> Many current Camera Module devices are available without the IR (infrared) filter. These are able to record better in low light conditions in conjunction with an external IR lamp (but daylight images have curious colours). These models are marked as 'NoIR'.

Raspberry Pi High Quality Camera

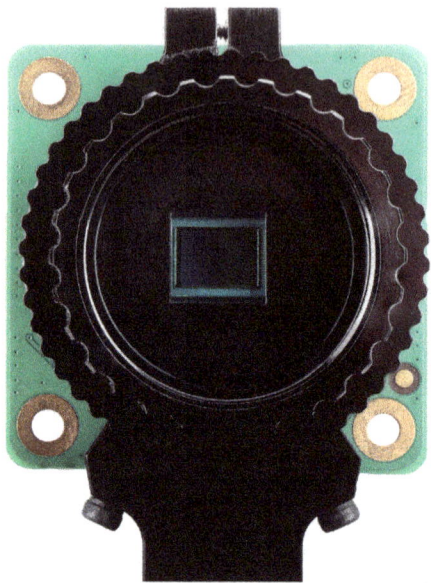

Figure 1-3   Raspberry Pi HQ Camera

Raspberry Pi High Quality (HQ) Camera (**Figure 1-3**), introduced in 2020, is larger and supports interchangeable C- and CS-mount lenses. It ships without an included lens. We recommend a wide-angle 6mm CS-mount lens and a narrower field of view 16mm C-mount lens; both are low cost and versatile. For specific applications, you may want more appropriate lenses. An alternative version of the HQ Camera that accepts M12 lenses was released in 2023. For more information, see "Using interchangeable lenses" on page 7.

The High Quality camera features a 12MP sensor offering a maximum resolution of 4032×3040 pixels, and because of its physically larger sensor size can be expected to produce better image quality than the Camera Module 2. It makes use of Sony's IMX477 image sensor and is also suitable for capturing video. At lower resolutions it can run at up to 120 frames per second.

 Removing IR

Some users have removed the IR (infra red) filter from the High Quality Camera. The operation requires some skill and will void any warranty and there's a significant risk of permanently destroying your camera.

Raspberry Pi Camera Module 3

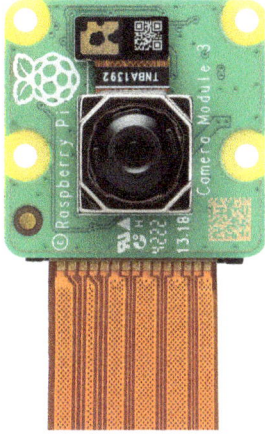

Figure 1-4 Camera Module 3

Introduced in 2023, the Camera Module 3 (**Figure 1-4**), is another small form factor camera similar to Camera Module 2. It offers increased resolution in a wider aspect ratio, an autofocus lens and support for HDR (High Dynamic Range) images. Note that the autofocus mechanism can be susceptible to vibrations in some adverse environments.

The autofocus can run in continuous mode, or be triggered prior to image capture, according to the software being used.

The maximum resolution of the sensor is 4608×2592 pixels, therefore note that it has a 16:9 rather than a 4:3 aspect ratio. Because of the special nature of this sensor, the HDR feature is not available at the maximum resolution, but only at a resolution of 2304×1296 pixels.

The sensor is quite capable for still photography, but shines particularly for video recording, particularly where HDR is beneficial. At an appropriate resolution it will support video capture at up to 120 frames per second.

Based on the Sony IMX708 sensor, it is packaged into four different variants:

- **Camera Module 3** — The regular version with an IR filter and lens with the standard field of view
- **Camera Module 3 Wide** — A version with an IR filter but replacing the standard lens with a wide angle one
- **Camera Module 3 NoIR** — A version without an IR filter but with the standard field of view lens

- **Camera Module 3 NoIR Wide** — A version without an IR filter and with the wide angle lens

Raspberry Pi Global Shutter Camera

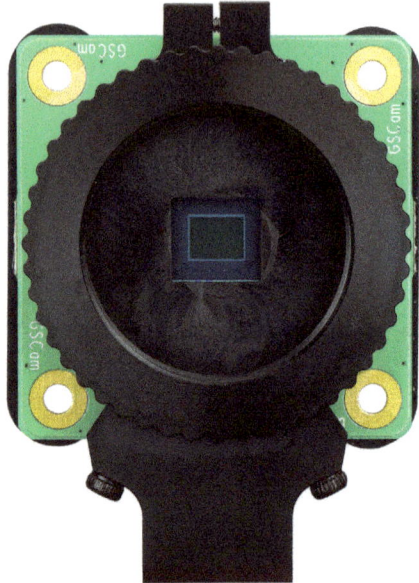

Figure 1-5   Global Shutter Camera

The Global Shutter (GS) camera (**Figure 1-5**), introduced in 2023, uses a different technology to the other cameras. Whereas it's normal in this market segment to use a *rolling shutter* camera, the GS camera has a *global shutter*.

This camera exposes all the pixels in an image at exactly the same time, rather than line by line as with the rolling shutter. This is great for capturing motion — the bus whizzing by in your video will remain a rectangle with the GS camera, whereas rolling shutter sensors will turn it into a parallelogram.

The GS camera is based on Sony's IMX296 image sensor. Global shutter cameras are electronically more complex so resolutions are generally lower. In this case, the GS camera produces 1456×1088 pixels, though on the upside, the extra internal complexity means that the physical pixels are larger, making the camera more sensitive and better at low light imaging. The GS camera uses the same mounting and lenses as the HQ camera.

Using interchangeable lenses

The HQ and GS cameras both use the same formats of interchangeable C-mount and CS-mount lenses. An adapter for M12 lenses is also available.

Raspberry Pi supplies a low-cost wide angle 6mm CS-mount lens and a larger 16mm C-mount lens (**Figure 1-6**). Their usage is identical except that the 16mm C-mount lens will require the C-CS adapter to be fitted first.

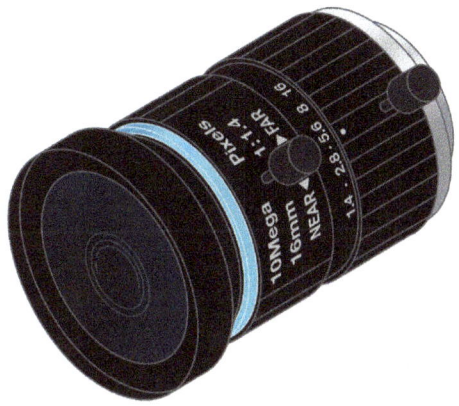

Figure 1-6   Raspberry Pi 16mm lens mount

Fitting the C-CS adapter

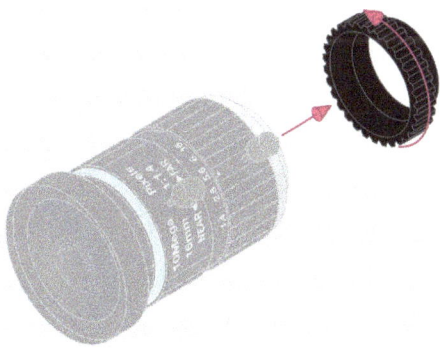

Figure 1-7   Fitting the C-CS adaptor to the 16mm lens

If you need the C-CS adapter (**Figure 1-7**), ensure that it is fitted to your 16mm lens. The lenses have a longer back focus than the 6 mm lens and therefore require the adapter.

Fitting the lens to the camera

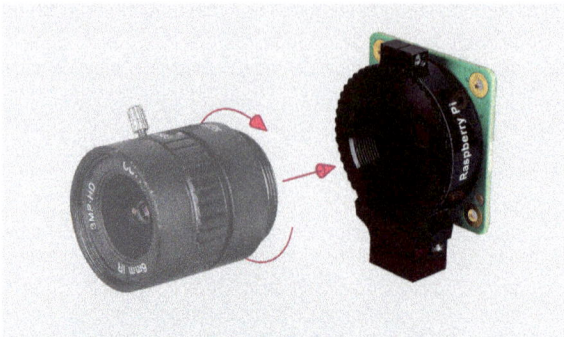

Figure 1-8 Rotate the lens clockwise

Rotate the lens (and C-CS adapter if present) clockwise all the way into the back focus adjustment ring (**Figure 1-8**).

Back focus adjustment ring and lock screw

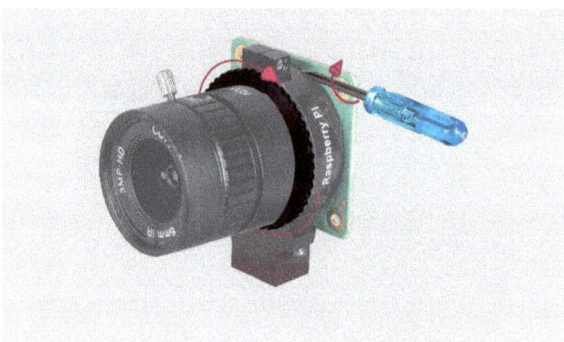

Figure 1-9 Screw the back focus ring in fully

The back focus adjustment ring should be screwed in fully. Use the back focus lock screw to make sure it does not move out of this position when adjusting the aperture or focus (**Figure 1-9**).

Aperture

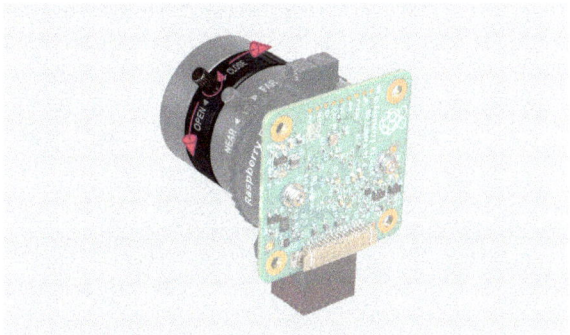

Figure 1-10 Adjust the aperture

To adjust the aperture, hold the camera with the lens facing away from you. Turn the inner ring, closest to the camera, while holding the camera steady. Turn clockwise to close the aperture and reduce image brightness. Turn anti-clockwise to open the aperture. When you're happy with the light level, tighten the screw on the side of the lens to lock the aperture into position, as shown in **Figure 1-10**.

Focus

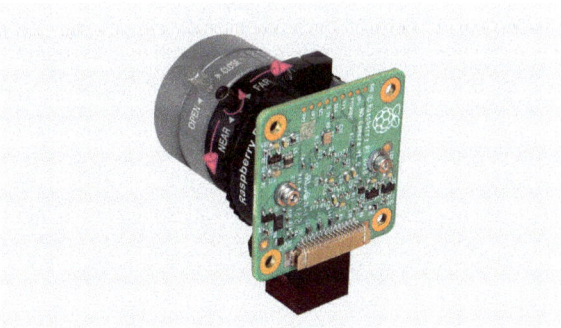

Figure 1-11 Adjusting the focus ring

To adjust focus, hold the camera with the lens facing away from you. Turn the focus ring (**Figure 1-11**), labelled **NEAR<>FAR**, anti-clockwise to focus on a nearby object. Turn it clockwise to focus on a distant object. You may find you need to adjust the aperture again after this.

Connecting and testing your camera

Your Raspberry Pi and camera are connected using a flat ribbon cable. There are two types of camera connector, the standard one which we find on all the camera boards and on older 'large' Raspberry Pi computers (Raspberry Pi 2, 3 and 4). Then there is a slightly narrower version of this connector which we find on 'small' Raspberry Pi computers (Raspberry Pi Zero, and Zero 2), on the Raspberry Pi 5, and also often on Raspberry Pi's I/O board that goes with the various compute modules.

Correspondingly, the cables may have both ends the same, or you can also get cables with one narrow end and one wider end.

On one side of the cable, the electrical connections, visible as narrow silver or golden stripes will be visible. On the other side, they are covered by a coloured (often but not always blue) piece of plastic. We'll refer to these as the *electrical* and *insulated* sides of the ribbon cable respectively.

Connecting to the camera

At the bottom of every camera board is a connector for the ribbon cable. At the edges you'll be able to grip the bottom part of the connector and pull it slightly out. Once you've done this you should be able to push the ribbon cable in. Finally, push those edges of the connector home again so that the ribbon cable is held firmly (**Figure 1-12**).

On all Raspberry Pi camera boards, the ribbon cable must be inserted so that the electrical side of the cable faces forwards. So, if you turn the camera board to point away from you, so that you can't see the actual camera lens, then you should see the insulated side of the ribbon cable.

The camera ribbon cables are short for a reason — they can otherwise be prone to interference and transmission errors. We would generally recommend avoiding lengths greater than about 30 cm, though people have had success with longer cables too.

Connecting to Raspberry Pi

Raspberry Pi 5 and Raspberry Pi Zero boards have a narrower version of the connector, and therefore also need a ribbon cable with the narrower end. These are very similar, only smaller, and open and close in the same way. But do take care as they are more fragile and break more easily (**Figure 1-13**)

Large Raspberry Pi computers prior to the Raspberry Pi 5 have the same connector as you will find on the camera, and you can open and close it in the same

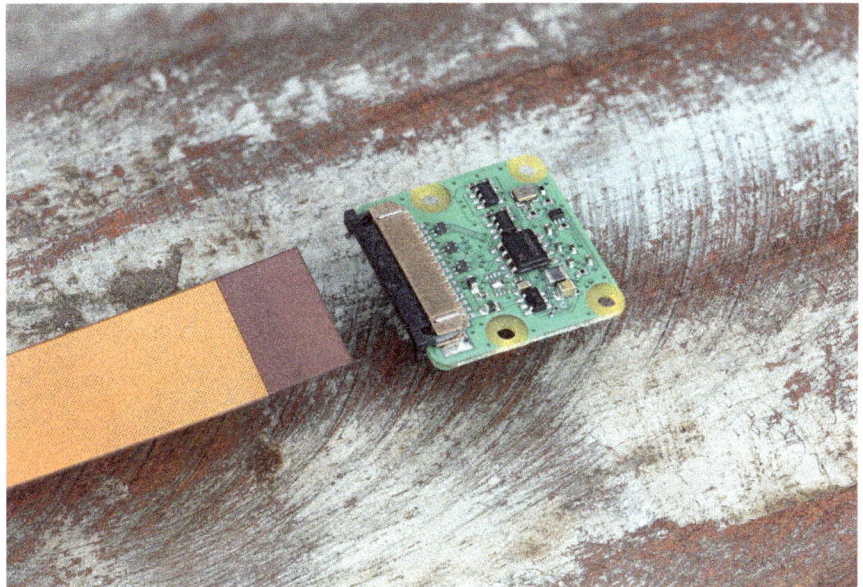

Figure 1-12 Connecting the ribbon cable

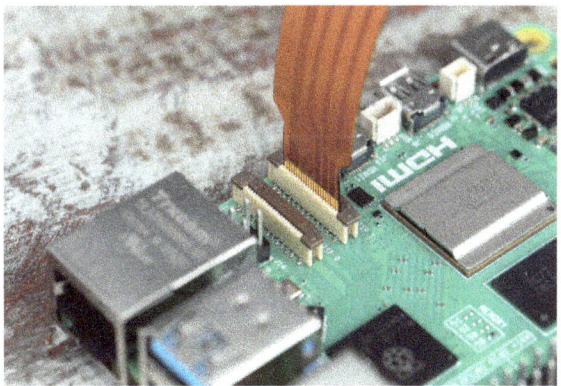

Figure 1-13 Connecting to Raspberry Pi

way. Note that there are two identical connectors on the boards — be sure to use the one located near the Ethernet and USB ports and not the one on the far side of the board. The ribbon would fit here but the camera will not function.

As for orientation, the insulated side of the ribbon cable must face towards the Ethernet and USB ports, so the electrical side will face towards the power connector.

When you insert the ribbon cable, make sure that the insulated side of the cable is face up. That is, when you can see the chips and connectors on the top of the board, you can also see the insulated side of the cable.

Some other boards, such as the I/O board Raspberry Pi makes for Compute Modules, have a different version of the narrow connector. This version is hinged — carefully prise the edge of it up. The ribbon cable should be inserted with the electrical side face down. The hinged part of the connector should now be snapped shut on top of the insulated side of the connector.

When using a ribbon cable with a wide and a narrow end, be sure to use the cable supplied with the camera, or one which states explicitly that it is a camera cable. There are display cables that have the same connectors but with a different pinout, and these and will not work.

Test your camera

To test that your camera is correctly connected and working, you'll need to install Raspberry Pi OS (Operating System) onto your board. Using Raspberry Pi Imager (**magpi.cc/imager**), write Raspberry Pi OS to a microSD card. We recommend choosing the 64-bit version of the operating system for devices with at least 1GB of memory (Raspberry Pi 3, 4 and 5) and the 32-bit version for devices with less memory (Pi Zero W, Pi Zero 2W and early models).

Insert this into your Raspberry Pi and power it on. Let it perform all the necessary updates when it first boots and then finally reboot it again.

For those less familiar with Raspberry Pi computers, we would recommend performing your initial testing with a keyboard and screen attached directly to your Raspberry Pi. Using the Raspberry menu, open the Accessories category and click on the Terminal button. Into the Terminal window it should be sufficient to type:

`rpicam-hello`

This will open a camera preview window and display the camera images there for about five seconds (**Figure 1-14**). If you don't see the preview window, please check that:

- You are connected to your Raspberry Pi with a screen and keyboard

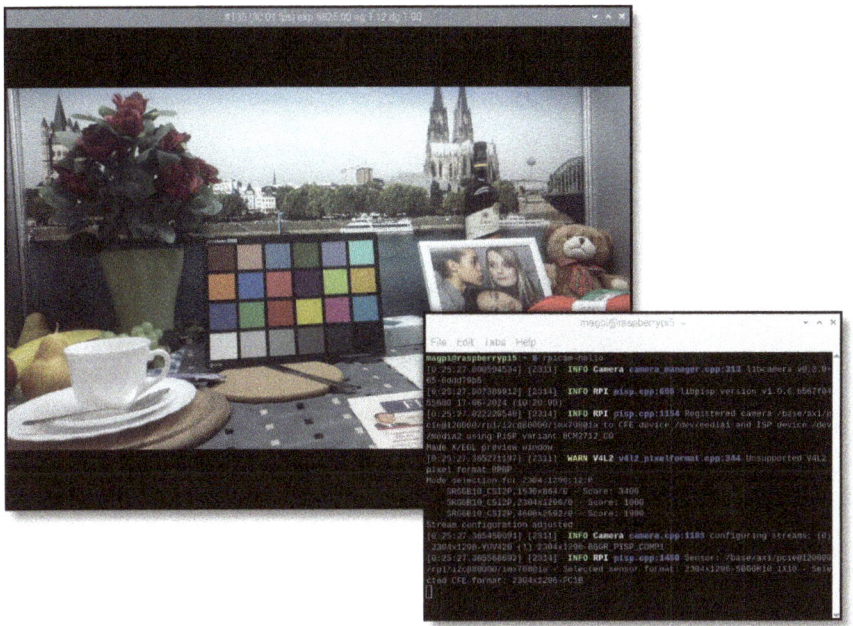

Figure 1-14   Testing the camera with rpicam-hello

▸ You are running the official Raspberry Pi software and that it is fully up to date. If you have made any changes to your Raspberry Pi's configuration please consider reverting back to the standard unaltered Raspberry Pi OS (by re-writing your micro SD card if necessary) and trying again

▸ All your cables are the right way round and seated correctly

▸ You are using an official Raspberry Pi camera. Non-official cameras are supported, but may need some extra configuration which the module vendor would have to supply

▸ You have a good quality power supply. Raspberry Pi power supplies are recommended because they are known to supply sufficient power to Raspberry Pi and the camera

Please check out Raspberry Pi's Camera Forum (**magpi.cc/camera-forum**) for more tips if you're having trouble.

Capturing your first photo

Raspberry Pi OS comes with a number of command line utilities for capturing images in various different ways. We've already seen **rpicam-hello** which we used to test that the camera was working. The next one is **rpicam-still**. This opens up a camera preview window just like **rpicam-hello** did but once it's run for five seconds it will capture a high resolution still photograph as a JPEG file, and then quit (**Figure 1-15**). To use it like this, enter:

`rpicam-still -o picture.jpg`

Note how the **-o** option specifies the name of the file to which the image is saved. There is also the **-t** option which specifies how long, in milliseconds, the preview window runs before the image is captured. To capture the image after ten seconds of preview, use:

`rpicam-still -t 10000 -o picture.jpg`

You can view your pictures by double-clicking on the files you've saved in the File Manager. You'll learn about many more of **rpicam-still**'s options in the chapters that follow.

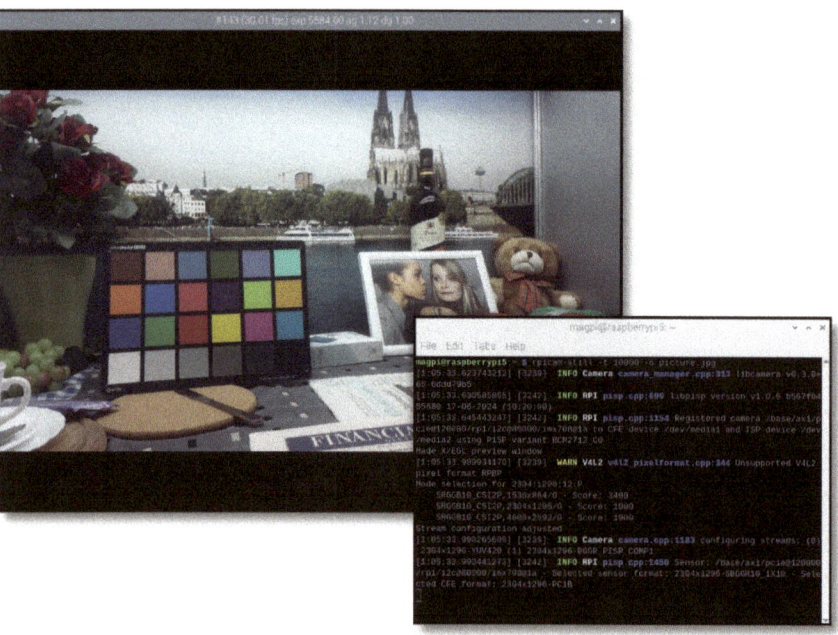

Figure 1-15   Using rpicam-still to capture an image

Capturing your first video

There's another command line tool for capturing videos, this time it's called **rpicam-vid.** You can use the **-o** and **-t** options as you did before, though this time **-t** specifies how long (again in milliseconds) the video lasts (**Figure 1-16**). To save a ten second video use:

`rpicam-vid -t 10000 -o video.h264`

Note that the file name ends with .h264 which identifies the format of the video file. Unfortunately, not all video players will play the .h264 format correctly, so we would recommend using a utility like **ffplay**. To play your video file with **ffplay**, type:

`ffplay video.h264`

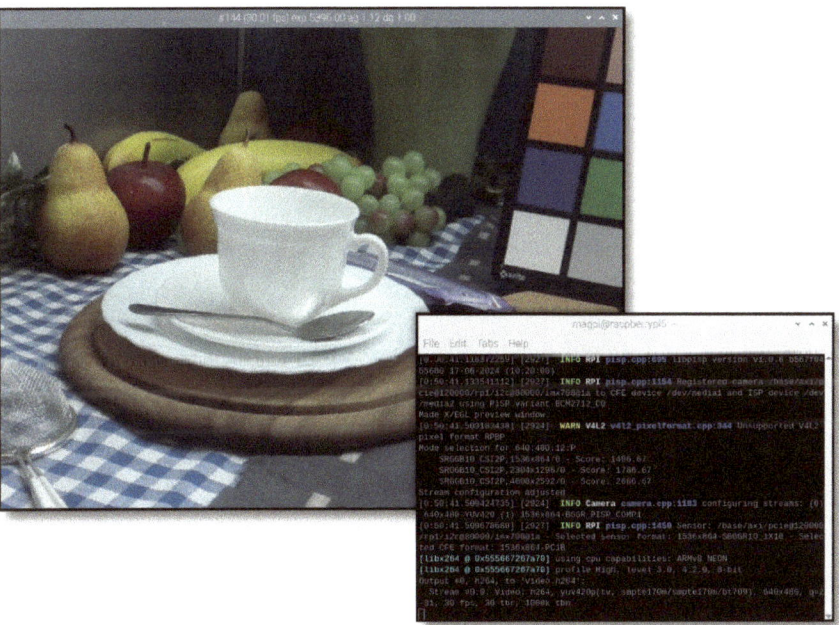

Figure 1-16   Using rpicam-vid to capture a video

You'll learn how to save different formats of video, as well as more of **rpicam-vid**'s advanced features, in the chapters that follow.

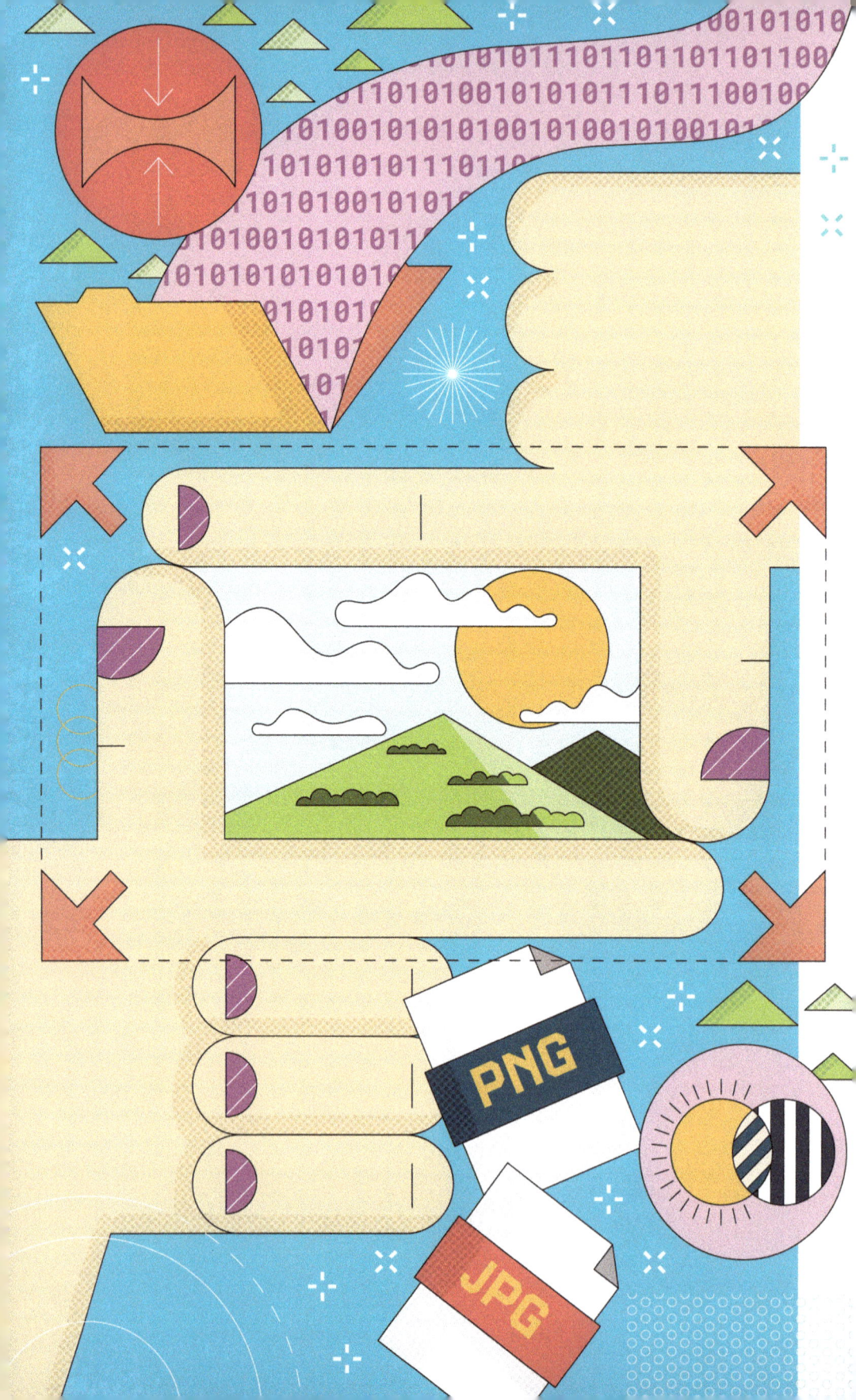

Chapter 2

More on still image capture

Resolutions, encoders, and file types

You've already met **rpicam-still** which allows you to capture still images. But it also has many more options controlling how it captures images, and the file formats and available image encoders. You'll discover some of those in this chapter. For now, we shall continue to assume that you have your keyboard and a monitor plugged directly into your Raspberry Pi.

Capturing images at different resolutions

By default, **rpicam-still** will capture images at the maximum available resolution supported by the camera. For the HQ camera, for example, this means images that are 4056×3040 pixels in size. But it's easy to change this with the **--width** and **--height** parameters (**Figure 2-1**). For example, if you want to capture an image that is 1536×1024 pixels instead, you should use:

```
rpicam-still --width 1536 --height 1024 -o smaller.jpg
```

Image encoders and file formats

Images are normally encoded in some way (often they are compressed so that they aren't so large) and then saved to a standard file format on the disk.

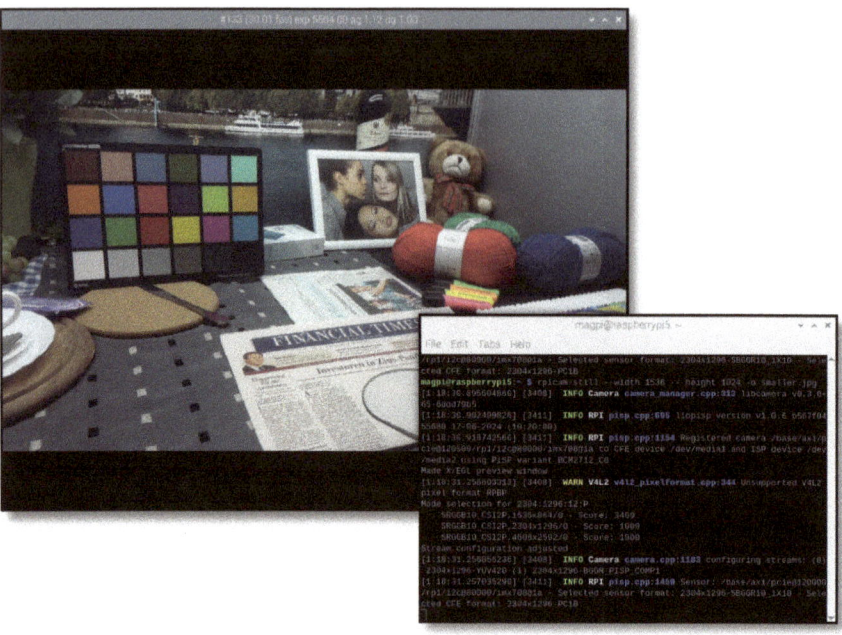

Figure 2-1   Capturing an image using the `--width` and `--height` parameters

JPEG files

The default file format used by `rpicam-still` is JPEG because of the very wide support that it has, combined with a useful level of compression. Usually, JPEG files are given the extension **.jpg**, or sometimes **.jpeg**.

JPEG is a lossy compression format, meaning that the result of loading your JPEG file is no longer identical to the image that you started from, though the differences are arranged to be ones that you will least notice. In return, you get to specify a quality factor indicating how much compression you want. At very low values your image will indeed deteriorate, but at very high values the JPEG process will be visually lossless, that is, it really will look as good as the original camera image.

The quality factor ranges from 1 to 99, and if you don't give one it will choose the value 93, which equates informally to "quite high quality". To save a JPEG at a different quality level, use the `-q` (or equivalently `--quality`) parameter like this:

`rpicam-still -q 80 -o test.jpg`

Please experiment with quality values like 10 and 50 to see what you get! See **Figure 2-2** and **Figure 2-3** for examples of the differences.

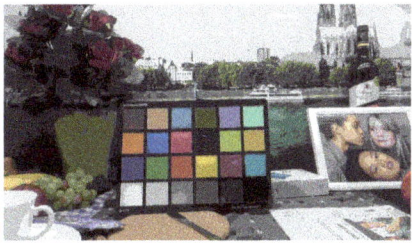

Figure 2-2
An image captured with the **-quality** parameter set to **10**

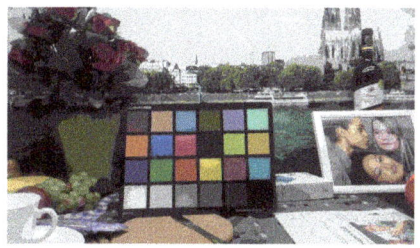

Figure 2-3
An image captured with the **-quality** parameter set to **50**

PNG files

PNG (or 'Portable Network Graphic') is another file and compression format which enjoys wide support. PNG is a lossless compression format, meaning that you are guaranteed to be able to recover exactly the same image that you started from (unlike JPEG). On the downside, PNG files are normally larger than JPEG files, and your Raspberry Pi has to work harder work to create them, which takes longer. **Figure 2-4** shows a captured PNG file.

To save a PNG file you'll need to tell **rpicam-still** that you want to use a different encoder using the **-e** or **--encoder** parameter, like this:

`rpicam-still -e png -o test.png`

Note that it's necessary to specify the **-e** option to get a PNG file — changing the file name on its own is not enough. PNG does not support a quality parameter.

DNG files

DNG, or 'Digital NeGative', files are quite different from PNG files despite the similar abbreviation! As the full name suggests, they're somewhat analogous to the negatives we had from film cameras before developing them into photos. In our case, the DNG file stores the raw numbers received from the image sensor before the hardware on Raspberry Pi 'develops' it into a viewable (JPEG or PNG) image. DNG files are saved alongside the 'developed' JPEG or PNG version of the same image. To save a DNG file, use the **-r** (or **--raw**) parameter (see **Figure 2-5**):

`rpicam-still -r -o test.jpg`

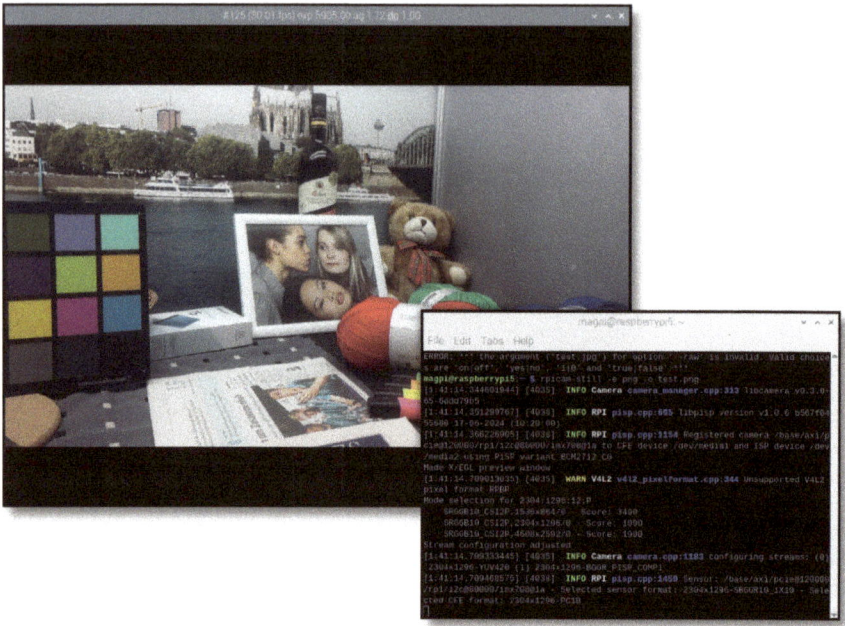

Figure 2-4   Capturing an image as a PNG file

`rpicam-still` will automatically replace **.jpg** by **.dng** in the DNG file name, giving both **test.dng** and **test.jpg** in this case.

Many third party software programs exist to 'develop' these DNG files interactively — a rather complex procedure beyond the scope of this guide.

Time-lapse captures

A time-lapse capture is where we capture an image at regular intervals, perhaps every minute, hour or day, and then reassemble them into a video where we play them back at a much faster rate. `rpicam-still` is all set up to capture the images we need out of the box.

We need to introduce the `--timelapse` option and we'll review a couple that you've seen before:

`-t` or `--timeout`

> The length of time in milliseconds for which to perform a capture. In the case of timelapse, `rpicam-still` will run capturing images in total

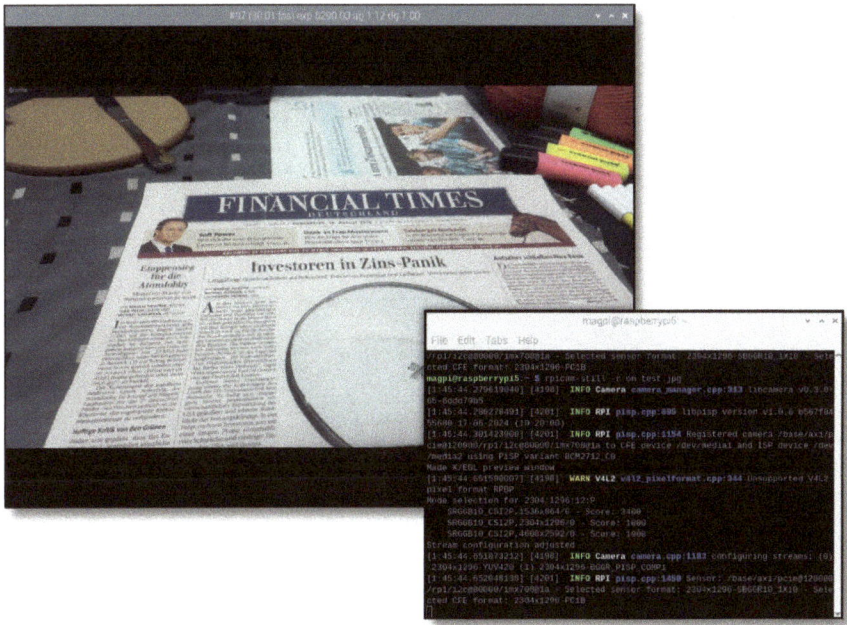

Figure 2-5 Capturing a DNG file

for this duration. You can pass the value 0 which means "run indefinitely" (you will have to stop **rpicam-still** manually, for example by pressing **CTRL+C** on the keyboard).

--timelapse

The length of time, again in milliseconds, between each timelapse capture.

-o or **--output**

The name of the output file or files. For timelapse captures, we can't give all the images the same name, so we use a special syntax that includes an image counter. For example, **-o capture_%04d.jpg** means that all the files are named **capture_**, followed by a counter, and then **.jpg**. **%04d** specifies how the counter is formatted, in this case the 0 means to add leading zeroes to the number and the 4 means "so that every number has at least 4 digits". This is useful so that listing your image files will return them to you in chronological order.

Let's try an example:

```
rpicam-still -o capture_%04d.jpg --timelapse 5000 -t 30000 \
    --width 1024 --height 768
```

This will run for 30 seconds, capturing an image every 5 seconds, and they'll be called **capture_0000.jpg** through to **capture_0004.jpg**, as shown in **Figure 2-6**. Note how we've reduced the resolution of the images to something that is more appropriate to the final video that we want to create.

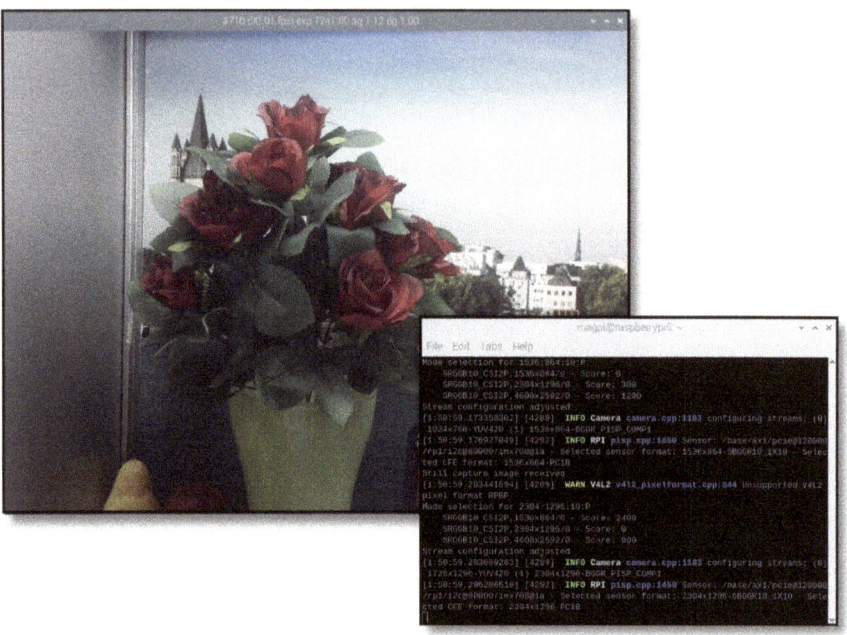

Figure 2-6 Capturing a timelapse

Assembling your images into a video

There's a handy tool called FFmpeg which is capable of turning your sequence of still images into a video. We can use it like this:

```
ffmpeg -r 2 -i capture_%04d.jpg video.mp4
```

Note how we format the name of the input files with the **%** syntax in the same way as we did for **libcamera-still**. The **-r** parameter gives the framerate of the output video, 2 frames per second in this case. We've chosen the MP4 format (which is generally well supported) and called it **video.mp4**.

FFmpeg is a versatile tool. Learn more about it at **magpi.cc/ffmpegdocs**.

Capturing when a key is pressed

Rather than doing regular captures, you can also do them in response to an event, or a key press. There are a couple of new option parameters to learn.

`--datetime`

Use this instead of `-o` to name the output file after the current date and time. The file will be named using the format **MMDDhhmmss.jpg** where **MM** and **DD** represent the month and date number, and **hh**, **mm** and **ss** are hours, minutes, and seconds.

`-k` or `--keypress`

Capture an image when **ENTER** is pressed on the keyboard. Press **X** and press **ENTER** to quit.

So the command to use is this:

`rpicam-still -t 0 --keypress --datetime`

Here you're running the capture indefinitely, so you'll have to type **X** followed by **ENTER** to quit (or press **CTRL+C**). Files would have names like 0405102742.jpg, meaning '10:27am, and 42 seconds, on 5 April'.

Capturing in response to a signal

Linux signals allow you to send a simple signal to a process that's running. This gives you an alternative to pressing a key and allows you to control `rpi-cam-still` from another process. To do this, replace `-k` (or `--keypress`) in the preceding command with `-s` or (`--signal`).

To send a capture signal to **rpicam-still**, start it with `-t 0 -s --datetime` and then type the following into another terminal window:

`kill -SIGUSR1 ` `` `pidof rpicam-still` ``

You can force **rpicam-still** to quit with:

`kill -SIGUSR2 ` `` `pidof rpicam-still` ``

Autofocus and High Dynamic Range

Autofocus is supported at the time of writing only on Raspberry Pi Camera Module 3. High Dynamic Range imaging is supported for all Raspberry Pi computers using Camera Module 3. Additionally, Raspberry Pi 5 is capable of High Dynamic Range imaging with other camera modules, but this topic lies beyond the scope of this guide.

Autofocus

When using the Camera Module 3, autofocus is enabled automatically in continuous mode. This means that the camera lens will move whenever necessary to maintain optimal focus on the centre part of the image, and this is probably what most users will want most of the time.

It's also possible to turn off autofocus and set the focus position of the lens manually. To do this, use the `--lens-position` parameter, and pass it a value measured in dioptres, meaning the reciprocal of the focus distance. Thus, to focus at a very close distance of about 0.1m, pass in the value 10 (which is 1 / 0.1). To focus at infinity, pass in 0 (informally, the value of 1 / infinity). You can pass in non-integer values too. For example:

```
rpicam-still --lens-position 0.5 -o infinity.jpg
```

...will set the focus position to approximately 2m (1 divided by 0.5) and not move the lens again.

High Dynamic Range Imaging

The Camera Module 3 supports High Dynamic Range (or HDR) imaging. To use it, specify the `--hdr` option on the command line, as in:

```
rpicam-still --hdr -o hdr.jpg
```

Figure 2-7 shows the result of capturing an image with HDR off, and **Figure 2-8** shows the results with HDR on.

Maximum HDR

Non-HDR captures can be performed at a maximum resolution of 4608×2592 pixels, but HDR captures, because of the special nature of the sensor required to support HDR, are limited to 2304×1296 pixels (exactly half the width and height of the non-HDR mode).

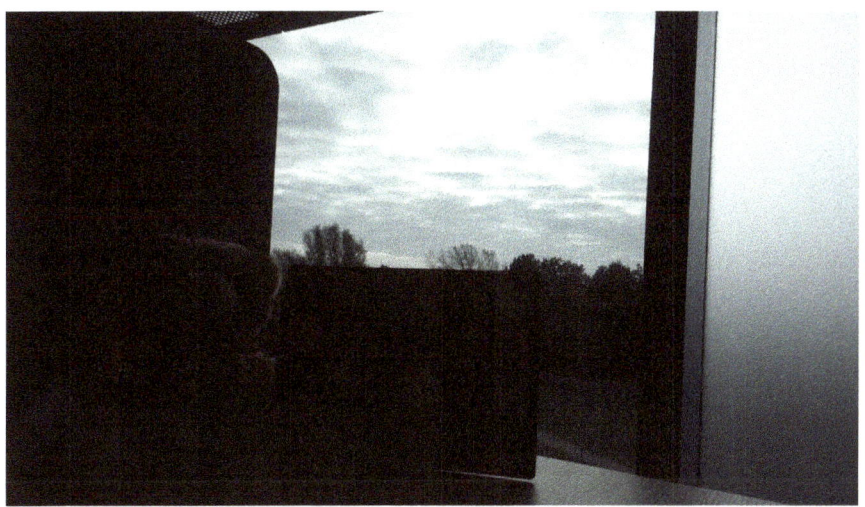

Figure 2-7 Capturing images with HDR off

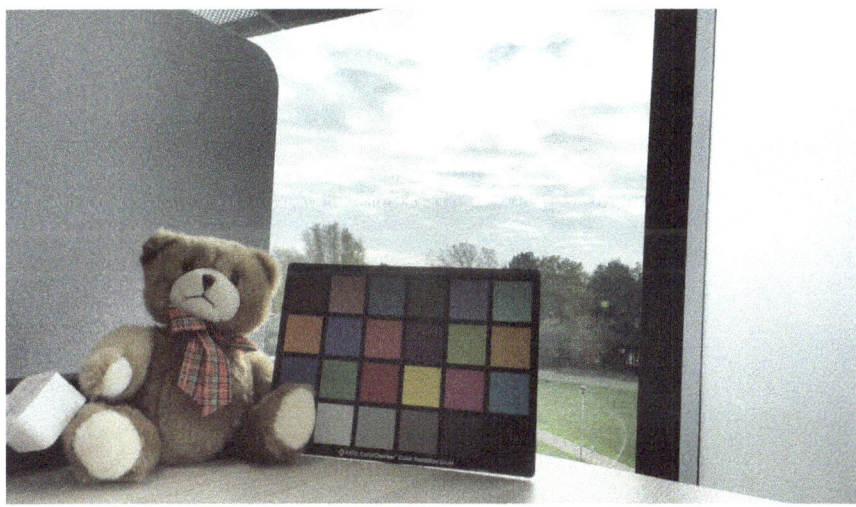

Figure 2-8 Capturing images with HDR on

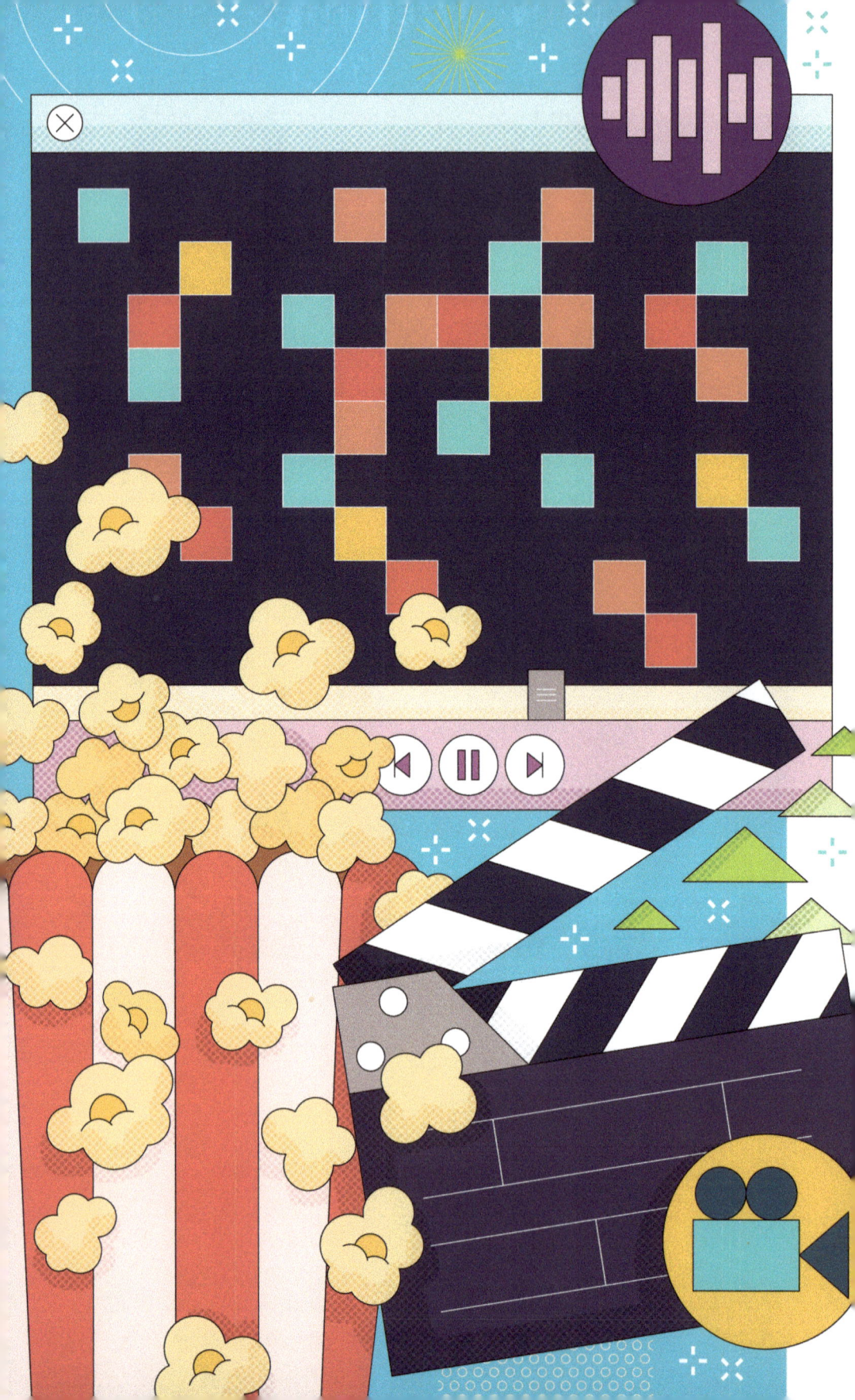

Chapter 3

More on Video Capture

Learn how to adjust video settings

You met **rpicam-vid** at the end of chapter one and found out how to record a short video clip. Like **rpicam-still**, **rpicam-vid** has many more options for controlling the resolution, framerate, and other aspects of the video that we capture, and you'll discover some of those in this chapter.

Changing the Video Resolution and Framerate

By default, **rpicam-vid** will capture videos at a resolution of 640×480 pixels. But it's easy to change this with the **--width** and **--height** parameters (just like **rpicam-still**). For example, if you want to capture a video that is 1920×1080 pixels (known as 'full HD') instead (**Figure 3-1**), please use:

```
rpicam-vid --width 1920 --height 1080 -o full_hd.h264
```

This particular resolution of 1920×1080 pixels should be regarded as the largest resolution that can be captured in video, unless noted otherwise.

Because you're working with videos now, you can also ask for different framerates. By default, **rpicam-vid** will deliver 30 frames per second (or fps). You can ask for a different framerate using the **--framerate** parameter:

```
rpicam-vid --width 1280 --height 720 --framerate 50 -o 50fps.h264
```

This will record a 720p video at 50fps, so long as the camera can deliver the frames that quickly (otherwise you will get the maximum framerate the camera can supply).

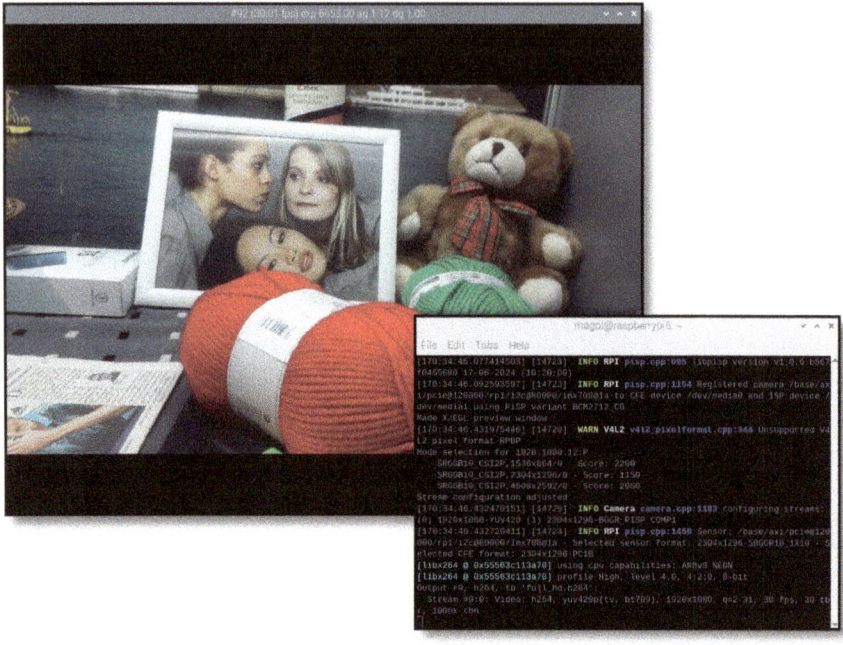

Figure 3-1   Capturing video in 'full HD'

Video Encoders and File Formats

Videos, just like still images, are normally compressed before saving them to disk. In fact, it's even more important to compress video frames because, with hundreds or thousands of frames, the output file will explode in size.

After compression, the video frames are written to a file with a specific *container format*. There's a choice as to how to organise video frames in a file, not least because there can be other data — such as audio — in the file too. The container format defines exactly how playback software can access and decode the information.

H.264 Files

The default encoder used by **rpicam-vid** is the H.264 video encoder. This combines both good performance and good compression. Once compressed, the frames are written back to back directly to a file which we normally describe as an *H.264* file, and by convention often denote it with the file extension .h264.

It's worth noting that these H.264 files are very simple; they're not really true container formats. That is, you cannot record audio data with the video, and the video frames do not even have timing information associated with them. Support for playing back such files can be limited, and even where it is supported, the software will have to guess a framerate for the video.

Popular media player software VLC used to support the H.264 file format but more recently no longer plays them correctly. For this reason, we recommend other programs, such as FFplay.

You've already seen how to record a video with a different resolution; another useful option is the bitrate parameter (**--bitrate** or just **-b**). This controls the size of the video file created, and therefore the amount of compression and the perceived quality. Consider the following command, which yields the results shown in **Figure 3-2**:

```
rpicam-vid -b 1000000 --width 1920 --height 1080 -o bad.h264
```

Compare that to the results of the following, shown in **Figure** 3-3:

```
rpicam-vid -b 9000000 --width 1920 --height 1080 -o good.h264
```

The 1,000,000 bits per second (1 megabit per second, or 1Mb/s) video (**bad.h264** option) shows far more objectionable compression artefacts than the 9 Mb/s 'good' video.

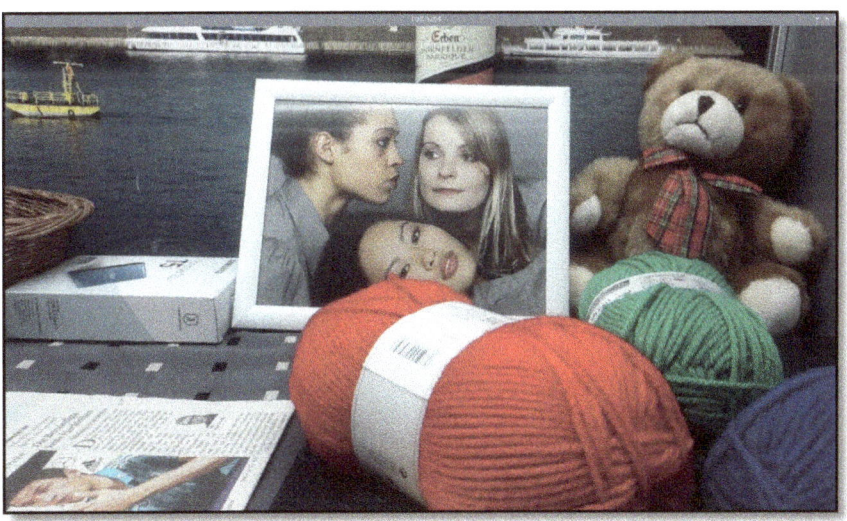

Figure 3-2 Video captured with a 'bad' bitrate

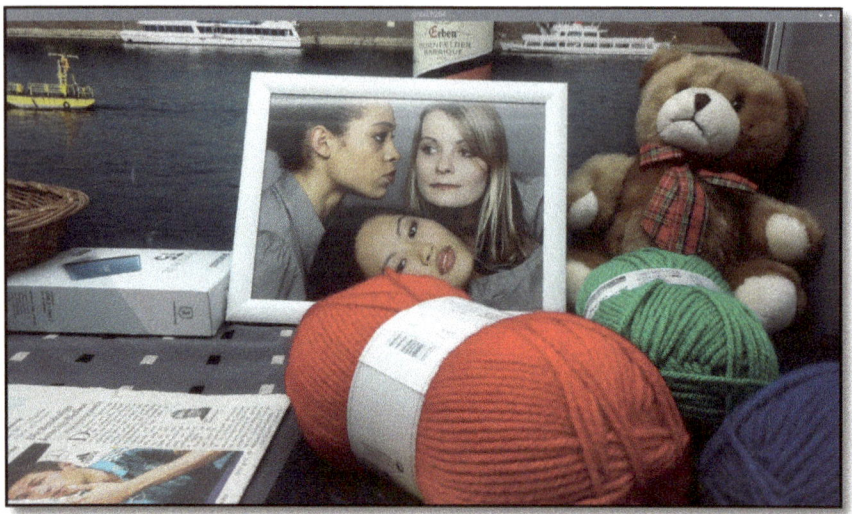

Figure 3-3 Video captured with a 'good' bitrate

MJPEG Files

You've previously encountered the JPEG image encoder for compressing still images. There's nothing to stop you from compressing one still image after another (very quickly) and saving them back to back to create a video file. That's exactly what an MJPEG file is.

There are some drawbacks, however. The MJPEG file format grew up organically and so lacks some clear decisions on exactly how to format the JPEGs within them. Often, they work well, but support can be a bit patchy.

To create and save a 20 second MJPEG file use this:

rpicam-vid -t 20000 --codec mjpeg -o test.mjpeg

You must specify the **--codec** option to get a proper MJPEG file — changing the file name on its own is not enough. Using the same JPEG encoder as **rpicam-still**, it supports the same JPEG quality parameter (**--quality** or **-q**), though in video files you can normally get by with lower values — indeed the default is only 50. An MJPEG file will ignore any setting made by **--bitrate** (or **-b**).

You can play an MJPEG file with **ffplay**:

ffplay test.mjpeg

MJPEG files, in contrast to H.264 files, can be recorded at resolutions greater than 1920×1080 pixels, though increasing the resolution will decrease the framerate at which **rpicam-vid** can keep up, resulting in dropped frames and possibly choppy videos.

Uncompressed Video Files

Most video compression formats are *lossy*, meaning that the video you save will have some degree of quality loss compared to the original camera images. Therefore, it's also possible to save completely uncompressed video, with the caveat that these files can become extremely large, and you would need to know exactly how you intend to use them.

To capture a compressed video use the **--codec yuv420** option as follows:

`rpicam-vid --width 320 --height 240 --codec yuv420 -o test.yuv420`

The relatively small size here (320×240 pixels) means the file size won't explode too rapidly, and also that the system won't get bogged down trying to write vast amounts of data to the disk (which can easily become quite slow).

Remember that, as usual, the **--codec** option is necessary and that changing the file name on its own is insufficient.

Finally, the format of the output file is a simple dump of each of the uncompressed image frames, one after the other. These are in 'YUV420 planar' format which you will need to understand in order to make use of it. The use of these files lies beyond the scope of this guide and is not recommended for beginners.

Uncompressed video files also have no resolution limit (as H.264 files do), though large resolutions will very quickly become a bottleneck due to the volume of data being written out.

MP4 Files, Audio and other Container Formats

You've seen that H.264 and MJPEG video files are not without certain limitations. A well-supported format is MP4, which **rpicam-vid** can create directly, even mixing in an audio stream if you have a microphone.

To create an MP4 file you have to choose a different codec. It will still use Raspberry Pi's hardware H.264 encoder but will access it via a third-party library that will take care of the MP4 container.

To record an MP4 file without audio, use: **rpicam-vid --codec libav -o test.mp4**

The usual options that you've seen so far (**--timeout**, **--width**, **--height**, and **--bitrate**) will all work as before, though the other options discussed later in this chapter won't (unless stated otherwise).

To create an MP4 file with an audio stream, use:

```
rpicam-vid --codec libav --libav-audio -o test.mp4
```

This will choose reasonable defaults for encoding the audio. The **libav** encoder can handle other container formats such as MKV files or MPEG2 Transport Streams. It is possible to stream the latter directly over a network. See our online documentation for more information (**magpi.cc/rpicamdocs**).

Pausing and Resuming Recordings

> This feature is not available when using a Raspberry Pi 5.

You could pause and resume recording by stopping **rpicam-vid** (for example with **CTRL+C**) and running it again when you want the recording to resume. This would leave you with many video files to stitch together. Instead, just as you can get **rpicam-still** to capture images when you press a key, you can get **rpicam-vid** to pause or resume a recording in the same way.

There are a few more options that we need to cover:

-t or **--timeout**

The length of time, in milliseconds, for which **rpicam-vid** will run. This will usually be zero if you're using **-k** or **--keypress** to terminate the application with a keypress.

-k or **--keypress**

Pressing the **ENTER** key toggles between recording and not recording. Type **x** and press **ENTER** to quit.

--initial pause or **--initial record**

This starts **rpicam-vid** in the paused (i.e. not recording) or recording state. Press **ENTER** to toggle between paused and recording.

--split

Every time a recording is resumed, the it writes a new output file.

--inline

Inserts extra header information at the start of every file that **rpicam-vid** writes. You should normally include this when using the **--split** option.

-o or **--output**

The name of the output file or files. With the **--split** option you'll often want a different name for each output file, so you can use the same *counter syntax* as **rpicam-still**'s timelapse option. For example, **-o vid_%03d.h264** creates **vid_000.h264**, **vid_001.h264**, **vid_002.h264**, etc.

Here's an example:

```
rpicam-vid -t 0 --inline --split --initial pause -k \
  --width 1280 --height 720 -o video_%03d.h264
```

This will start **rpicam_vid** in the paused state, so it won't be recording anything yet. When you press ENTER, it will start recording **video_000.h264**. It will pause when you press ENTER again, and then start recording **video_001.h264** when you press ENTER for the third time. This will carry on indefinitely until you press **x** followed by ENTER.

Recording in Response to a Signal

> This feature is not available when using a Raspberry Pi 5.

Linux allows you to send a simple *signal* to a process that's running. This alternative to pressing a key allows you to control **rpicam-vid** from another process. To do this, replace **-k** (or **--keypress**) with **-s** or (**--signal**).

To send a pause / record signal to **rpicam-vid**, use the preceding example, but replace **-k** with **-s** and then type the following into another terminal window:

```
kill -SIGUSR1 `pidof rpicam-vid`
```

And you can force **rpicam-vid** to quit with:

```
kill -SIGUSR2 `pidof rpicam-vid`
```

This should be familiar as it matches **rpicam-still**'s behaviour!

Other Recording Options

rpicam-vid has many other parameters and we'll look very briefly through a few of them here.

Circular Buffer Output

 This feature is not available when using a Raspberry Pi 5.

One useful feature is the ability to keep writing the recorded video stream to a buffer in Raspberry Pi's memory. This is a limited size, and when it fills up the earliest data in the buffer is evicted to make space for the new frames. When **rpicam-vid** exits, this circular memory buffer is flushed to the disk. This enables you to leave the camera running indefinitely, but to save only the last several seconds of data when some event occurs that stops the program.

Let's see an example:

```
rpicam-vid -t 0 --keypress --circular 8 --inline \
  --width 1280 --height 720 -o circular.h264
```

This will run indefinitely writing to a circular memory buffer, and when the user types **x** and **ENTER**, the program will quit after saving the last 8MB (megabytes) of data to the file **circular.h264**. The number after the **--circular** option determines the size (in megabytes) of this memory buffer.

You can use **--signal** (or **-s**) instead of **--keypress** if you prefer.

Timing Information

We remarked earlier how H.264 format files contain no timing information. **rpicam-vid** allows this information to be output to a separate file for later use or analysis.

Here we simply specify the **--save-pts** option followed by a filename where the frame times from the start of the video are stored in text form in units of milliseconds, for example:

```
rpicam-vid --save-pts timestamps.txt -o circular.h264
```

The file **timestamps.txt** will (for a 30 fps recording) start like this:

```
# timecode format v2
0.000
33.332
66.664
99.996
```

...and so on.

Autofocus and High Dynamic Range

Autofocus is supported at the time of writing only on Raspberry Pi Camera Module 3.

High Dynamic Range imaging is supported for all Raspberry Pi computers using Camera Module 3. Additionally, Raspberry Pi 5 is capable of High Dynamic Range imaging with other camera modules, but this topic lies beyond the scope of this guide.

The support mirrors that in `rpicam-still` very closely.

Autofocus

When using Camera Module 3, autofocus is enabled automatically in continuous mode. This means that the camera lens will move whenever necessary to maintain optimal focus on the centre part of the image, and this is probably what most users will want most of the time.

It's also possible to turn off autofocus and set the focus position of the lens manually. To do this, use the `--lens-position` parameter, and pass it a value measured in *dioptres*, meaning the reciprocal of the focus distance. Thus, to focus at a very close distance of about 0.1m, pass in the value 10 (which is 1 / 0.1). To focus at infinity, pass in 0 (informally, the value of 1 / infinity). You can pass in non-integer values too. For example:

```
rpicam-vid --lens-position 0.5 -o infinity.h264
```

...will set the focus position to approximately 2m (1 divided by 0.5) and not move the lens again.

High Dynamic Range Imaging

The Camera Module 3 supports High Dynamic Range (or HDR) imaging, as shown in **Figure 3-4**. To use it, specify the `--hdr` option on the command line, as in:

```
rpicam-vid --hdr -o hdr.h264
```

Note that non-HDR captures (**Figure 3-5**) can be performed at a maximum resolution of 4608×2592 pixels, but HDR captures, because of the special nature of the sensor required to support HDR, are limited to 2304×1296 pixels (exactly half the width and height of the non-HDR mode). H.264 video files are, in any case, limited to 1920×1080 pixels, so this restriction is often not relevant.

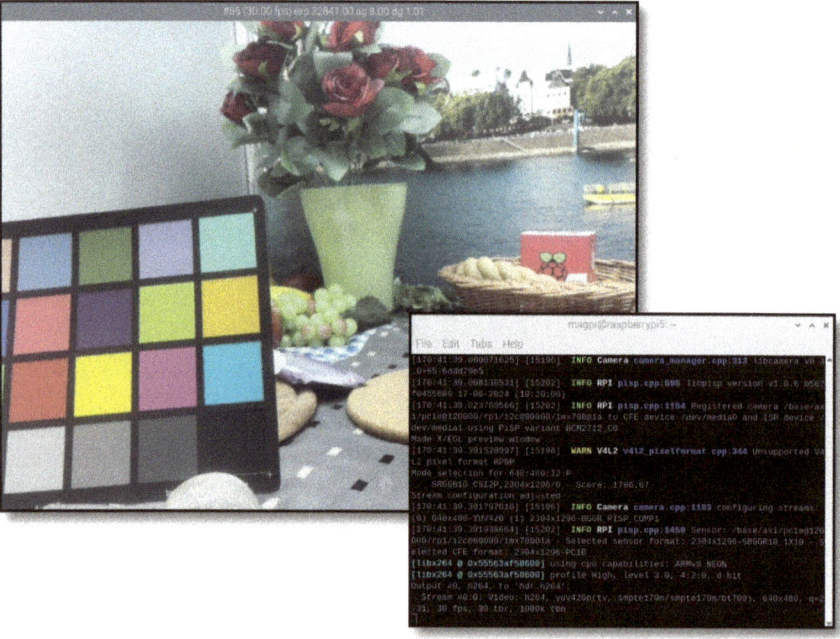

Figure 3-4 Capturing video in HDR

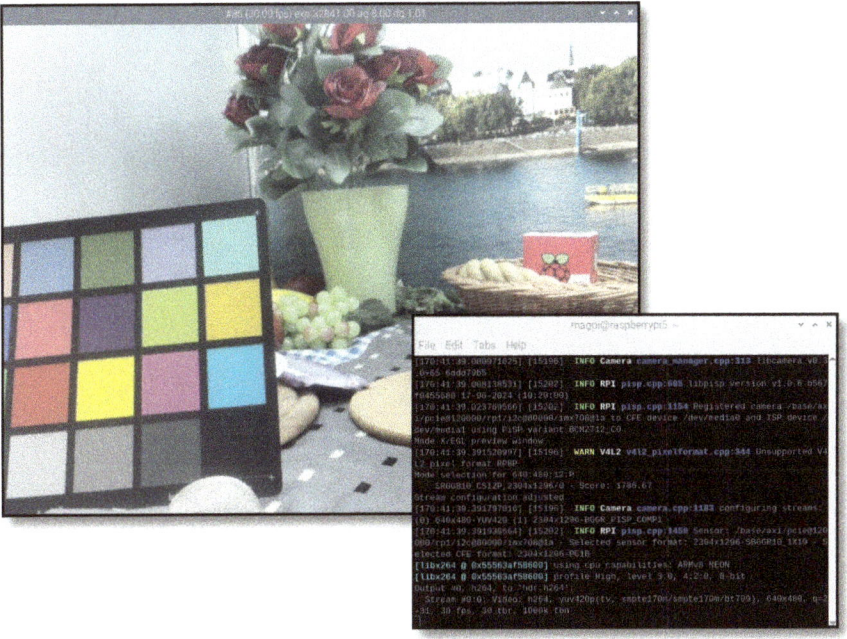

Figure 3-5 Capturing video in non-HDR

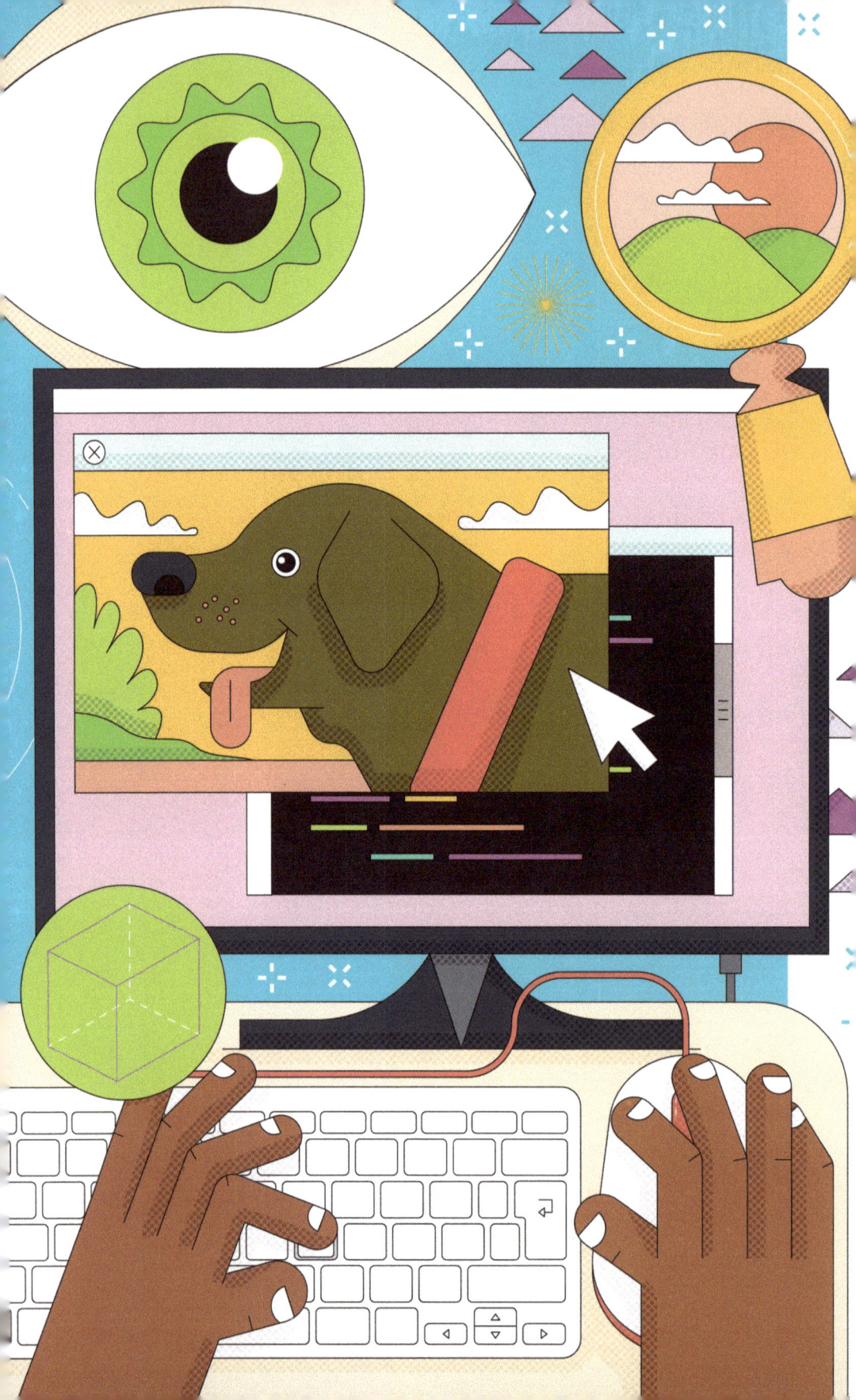

Chapter 4

Preview Windows

Get to know the different types of preview windows

So far, you haven't had to worry too much about the camera preview window. It just works. Nonetheless, you can exert some control over it, such as its size, and there are a few other tips worth knowing.

Types of Preview Window

There are three different types of preview window. Normally, the most appropriate type is chosen automatically, but there may be times when it's worth knowing about some of the others.

OpenGL Preview Window

When you're running Raspberry Pi OS with the desktop environment, and a display is connected directly to your Raspberry Pi with an HDMI cable, the OpenGL preview will open automatically.

It has the benefit of using the built-in 3D graphics hardware to optimise the rendering of the camera images, thereby leaving your device's CPU (Central Processing Unit) available for other tasks.

The OpenGL preview window does have some minor limitations. On Raspberry Pi 4 it won't be able to display a camera image that is more than 4096 pixels across. On lower-powered devices (such as Raspberry Pi 3), the limit is 2048 pixels. It would be unusual to create camera images wider than this for preview, so this doesn't normally pose a problem.

DRM Preview Window

When Raspberry Pi OS is not running in the desktop windowing environment (for example: when logging in directly to the console), then you will use the DRM preview window. If you are running the desktop environment, you can normally suspend it with **CTRL+ALT+F1** to drop out to the console environment, giving the same result (and use **CTRL+ALT+F7** to switch back).

DRM stands for *Direct Rendering Manager* and is a Linux interface for rendering to graphics devices. This is probably the most efficient way to render camera images to the screen as the task is taken over completely by your Raspberry Pi's display hardware. It is not related to the more commonly known *Digital Rights Management* which is used to control access to digital music and video files.

Unfortunately, the Raspberry Pi OS's desktop environment assumes sole control of the DRM interface which is why the DRM preview is only available when the desktop environment is not running or is suspended.

In this environment, obviously enough, the window has no title bar, nor is there any way to "grab" it and move it around the screen. When you are in the console environment, the DRM preview will open automatically.

Qt Preview Window

The Qt (pronounced "cute") preview window is in some respects similar to the OpenGL preview window in that it is available when running in the desktop environment. It's implemented using the Qt graphical user interface (GUI) toolkit, but the principal difference, from our point of view, is that the rendering is done in software (by the CPU) and not by the dedicated 3D graphics hardware. Because of this, normally the Qt preview window is a bad idea, but you may want to use it if:

- You're logged in remotely using **ssh**.
- You're viewing Raspberry Pi's desktop remotely using **vnc**.

When logged in remotely using ssh, you can forward the preview window to the machine where you are sat, rather than show them on a locally attached monitor (if there is one). You'll need to log in with X forwarding enabled, as in:

ssh -X user@your_pi

...replacing **user@your_pi** by the correct login for your own device.

Now you need to add `--qt-preview` to the command line of the rpicam application that you wish to use. All the applications behave identically in this respect. So, if you only want to see the camera images use:

`rpicam-hello --qt-preview`

In the case of vnc, the Qt preview window (**Figure 4-1**) sometimes runs more smoothly than the OpenGL one, though note that you will be causing a lot of uncompressed video traffic on your network.

Because of the Qt preview window's expense in terms of CPU, it is by default opened with quite a small size.

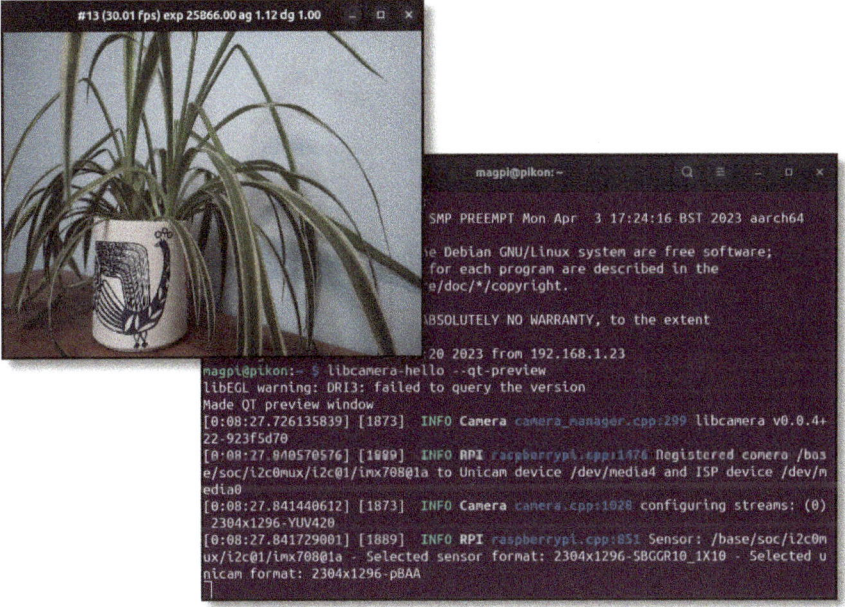

Figure 4-1   Using the Qt preview window instead of the default OpenGL preview window

Preview Window Options

You have a few command line options to control the behaviour of the preview window. Let's review those here.

--qt-preview

> Force the use of the Qt preview window when the OpenGL version would normally have been used.

`-n` or `--nopreview`

> No preview window is shown at all (though the camera runs normally). This can be helpful if you simply don't have a display where you can show images, and also in helping very high framerate video to avoid frame drops.

`-f` or `--fullscreen` [OpenGL preview only]

> Causes the OpenGL preview window to run in fullscreen mode (normally it runs in a regular medium-sized window).

`-p` or `--preview`

> (Followed by four comma-separated numbers, without any spaces.) This sets the size of the preview window. The four numbers are the x offset, y offset, width and height for the preview window.

Let's see a few examples:

`rpicam-vid --nopreview -o test.h264`

> This records a video without showing an on-screen preview.

`rpicam-hello --fullscreen`

> Show the camera preview in fullscreen mode.

`rpicam-hello --preview 100,100,1200,800`

> Show the camera preview in a 1200x800 pixel window, offset 100 pixels in both directions from the top left corner of the screen.

`rpicam-hello --preview 100,100,1200,800 --qt-preview`

> As above, but force the *Qt* preview window to be used. You may want to watch the output of the **top** command while this is running, and compare it with the results when you omit `--qt-preview`.

Obtaining Live Status Information

If you're using the OpenGL or Qt preview windows, the camera system can show live status information on the window's title bar. There is already a default selection, showing the current exposure time and gain, and some other things. But you can choose your own values using the `--info-text` parameter.

For example, to display a *focus measure* (**Figure 4-2**) you could use:

`rpicam-hello -t 0 --info-text "Focus %focus"`

...which will display the string Focus followed by a number indicating how well focused the image is (as the number increases, your scene should come more into focus). This is particularly useful for the HQ camera, allowing the user to adjust the manual focus ring to the best position.

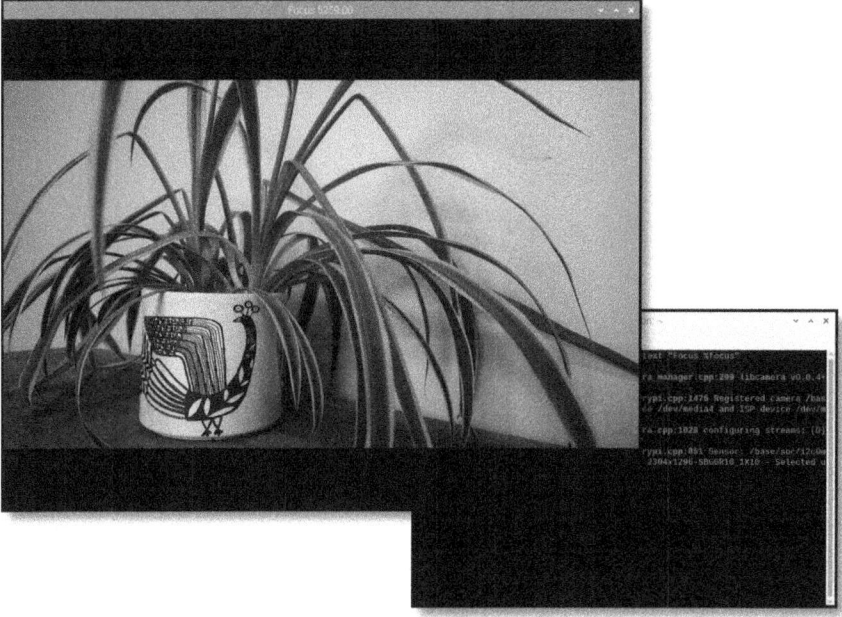

Figure 4-2 The preview window displaying a focus measure

In general, the `--info-text` parameter accepts a free-form text string where certain status fields, beginning with **%**, will be replaced by their live values. The available status fields are:

%frame

> A sequential count of the number of frames delivered.

%fps

> An instantaneous measure of the current frame rate (in frames per second).

%exp

> The exposure time of the current frame as reported by the sensor.

%ag

> The analogue gain of the current frame as reported by the sensor.

%dg

    The digital gain applied to the current frame.

%rg

    The gain applied to the red colour channel for white-balancing.

%bg

    The gain applied to the blue colour channel for white-balancing.

%focus

    A measure of sharpness (higher = sharper) which can be used for manual focus adjustment.

%aelock

    Whether the AE (auto exposure) algorithm thinks it has "settled".

%lp

    The current lens position (Camera Module 3 only).

%afstate

    The current state of the autofocus algorithm. It will report one of "idle", "scanning", "focused" or "failed" (Camera Module 3 only).

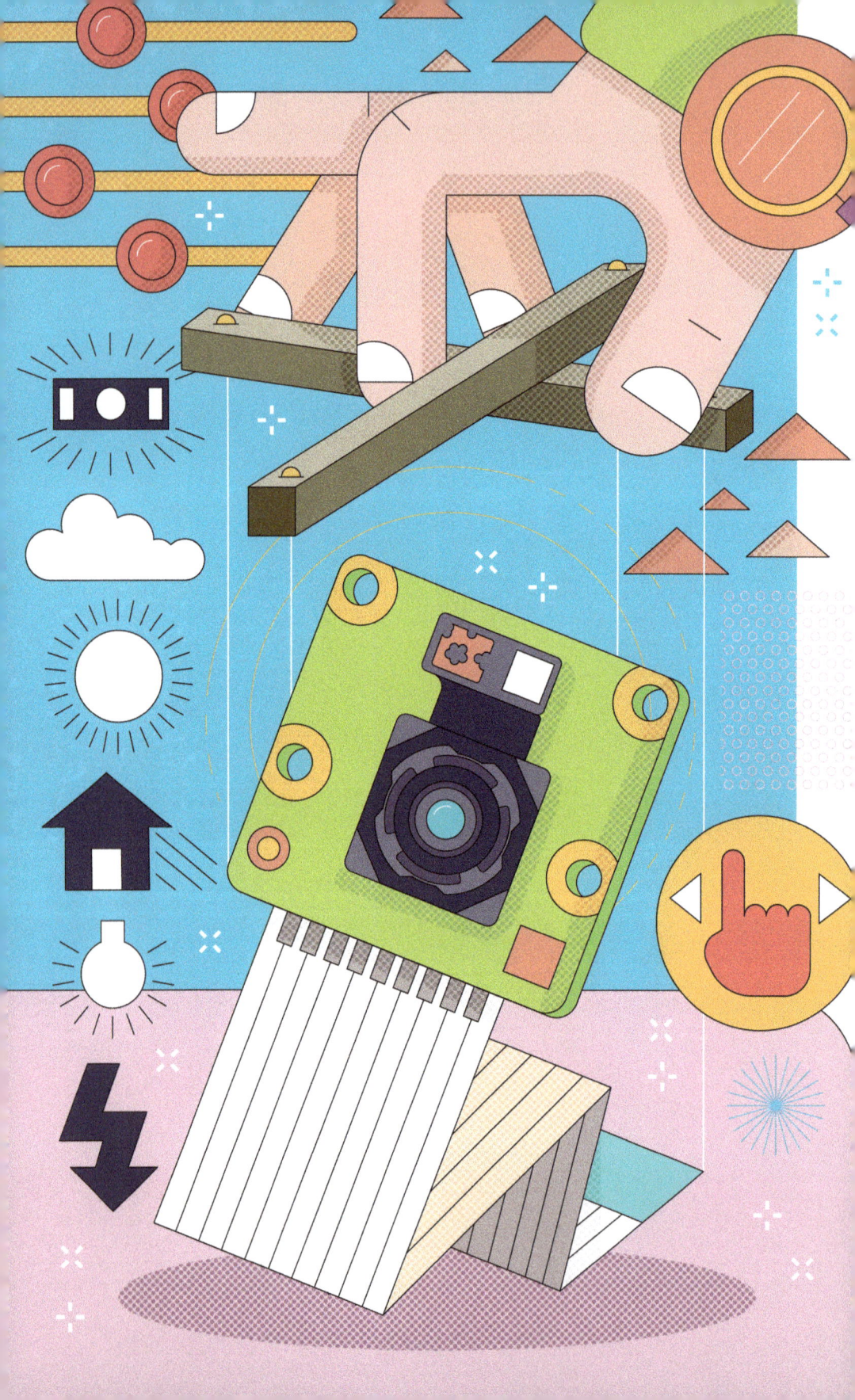

Chapter 5

Controlling the Camera

Learn how to adjust your camera settings

Previous chapters have spent some time explaining how to capture camera images in different ways, but we haven't yet shown how you can take control of the camera itself and the images that it delivers.

There are a number of different ways that you can control the behaviour of the camera, so we're going to divide them into three groups:

- **Image readout controls** — the orientation in which images are read out and how you can zoom into different parts of the image.

- **Camera controls** — various controls for the camera itself, such as the frame rate, exposure, white balance and autofocus.

- **Image processing controls** — finally, there are a number of options for how the captured images can be tweaked, such as increasing the sharpness, contrast or colour saturation of the image.

Image Readout Controls

Normally the camera system gives you images that are the right way up and the right way round: what's up appears up, and what's to the left of the camera's eye view is to the left. But there are occasions where a camera may be mounted upside-down, or perhaps there is a reason why an application may want a mirrored image.

Changing the Image Orientation

To mirror an image horizontally, use the option **--hflip**. This option applies identically to all rpicam applications, for example:

`rpicam-still --hflip -o mirrored.jpg`

Figure 5-1 shows an image captured naturally, and Figure 5-2 shows the flipped version.

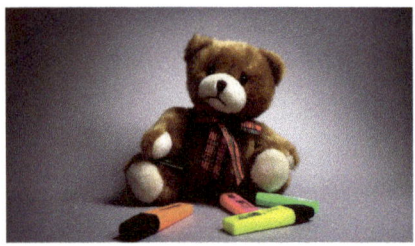

Figure 5-1
An image captured without the **--hflip** option

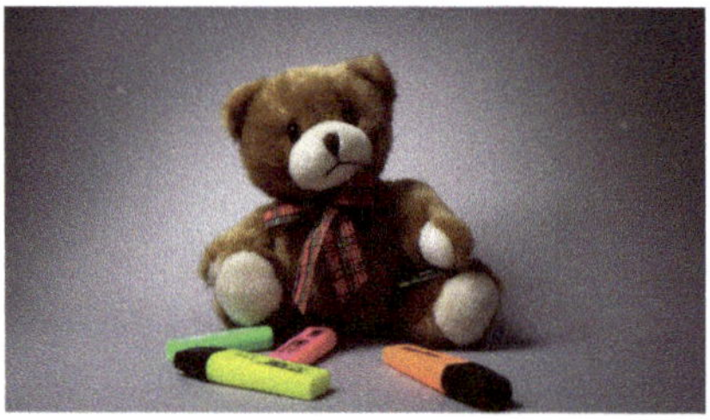

Figure 5-2
An image captured with the **--hflip** option

To flip an image vertically, use the **--vflip** option. You can use it in exactly the same way as **--hflip**.

To rotate an image 180 degrees you can specify both **--hflip** and **--vflip**, or you can use the option **--rot 180** which has the same effect, as in:

`rpicam-vid --rot 180 -o rotated.h264`

The rpicam applications are not able to rotate an image through 90 or 270 degrees. The easiest way to apply such a rotation to a captured image or video is to edit the file's metadata using a tool like exiftool (use **sudo apt install exiftool** to install it if needed). To rotate a JPEG image by 90 degrees use:

`exiftool -orientation="rotate 90" image.jpg`

Or use **"rotate 270"** to rotate the image anti-clockwise. To rotate an MP4 video through 90 degrees use:

`exiftool -rotation=90 video.mp4`

Use **-rotation=270** to rotate the video the other way.

> **H264 Rotation**
>
> It is not possible to rotate a **.h264** file in this way because, as discussed in "H.264 Files" on page 28, H264 is not a true container format.

Digital Zoom

Most cameras have a zoom feature. There are two types of zoom, namely *optical zoom*, which requires a zoom lens and *digital zoom* which works without a zoom lens by using digital up-scaling (this generally results in reduced quality).

Raspberry Pi cameras implement digital zoom by processing only a rectangular subset (a *crop*) of the pixels that is received from the image sensor. This crop is scaled back up to the full output size. By changing this crop you can zoom into the image, and even, by sliding it around, pan across the image.

The rpicam applications all allow you specify a *region of interest* parameter with **--roi**. This should be followed by a comma-separated list of 4 numbers:

x-offset

    The offset in the x-direction of the left hand edge of the crop from the left hand edge of the camera image

y-offset

    The offset in the y-direction of the top edge of the crop from the top edge of the camera image

width

    The width of the crop

height

    The height of the crop.

In all cases, the units are a proportion of the full camera image. So, if you wanted to zoom into the centre of the camera image with a scale factor of 2, you would use:

--roi 0.25,0.25,0.5,0.5

Notice how the values 0.25 cause the crop to be centred in the original image; if you had used zero instead in both places, you would be zooming into the top left corner of the original.

Let's finish with an example:

```
rpicam-hello --roi 0.25,0.5,0.333,0.333
```

This will zoom in by a factor of 3 onto an area where the top left pixel is a quarter of the way across the full camera image, and halfway down.

A useful tip is that to preserve the correct aspect ratio of the image, the width and height values should be the same (because they are relative to the original image from the sensor).

Camera Modes

Some image sensors may output images with a single resolution, and always showing the same field of view. Raspberry Pi cameras, however, generally give you a choice of resolutions. Sometimes these may all show the same field of view, or some of them may show a reduced field of view. Each of these is known as a *camera mode*. How do you know what camera mode you should be using?

Raspberry Pi's rpicam applications will all choose a camera mode for you based on the output image sizes that you request. However, the camera modes all have different trade-offs so it can't guarantee to get this right all the time.

Camera modes, therefore, are a somewhat tricky topic, and are the subject of Chapter 6, *Understanding Camera Modes*.

Camera Controls

Many consumer-grade digital cameras have familiar controls for things like the exposure time, the ISO (or gain, in a digital camera), the white balance and so on. All these are available for Raspberry Pi cameras too.

Controlling the Camera's Exposure

Normally the camera runs an automatic exposure algorithm, adjusting exposure time to produce images of reasonable brightness. But sometimes users may want images that are brighter or darker than the default.

Adjusting the Target Exposure

One convenient way to do this is with the **--ev** parameter. This parameter adjusts the target for the auto exposure algorithm in units of stops. The default value is 0, and adding 1 to the value doubles the brightness. Similarly, subtracting 1 halves the brightness, so it is a logarithmic scale. For example:

`rpicam-hello --ev 0.5`

...will increase the overall exposure by 0.5 stops, equivalent to √2, an increase of approximately 41%.

Changing the Exposure Mode

Normally, the camera system delivers the target overall exposure with a balanced choice of values for the camera's shutter speed and the camera's gain. In some situations, such as when capturing moving objects, it can be desirable to lower the time for which the shutter is open but to increase the gain to compensate.

This can be accomplished by requesting the **sport** exposure mode:

`rpicam-still --exposure sport -o action_shot.jpg`

Fixing the Shutter Speed and the Gain

In the end you always have the option to select your own values for the camera's shutter speed and gain. If you set just one of them, then the other will still be varied by the auto exposure algorithm so as to give you a reasonable exposure. But if you fix both, then the brightness of your images is completely determined and will never change.

The command line parameters to use are **--shutter** to set the time for which the image is being exposed (in units of microseconds), and **--gain** to set the gain value. Multiplying the two together yields the *total effective exposure*, so that any images with the same total effective exposure should be equivalently bright. Let's see an example:

`rpicam-still --shutter 9000 --gain 2.0 -o image.jpg`

This will capture an image that has been exposed for 9ms, and with an analogue gain of 2.0. There will be no variation of brightness, whatever the camera is pointed at.

Setting the Frame Rate

The cameras normally run at 30 frames per second (fps), but you can set a different value using the `--framerate` parameter, also in units of frames per second. For example, to run the camera at 15fps you could use:

rpicam-hello -t 0 --framerate 15

You can use non-integer numbers of frames per second too.

> **Frame Rate and Exposure**
>
> The frame rate implies an upper bound on the longest exposure that is possible. For instance, at a frame rate of 30fps, you won't be able to get exposure longer than 1/30 seconds, or about 33 milliseconds. In practice the limit will be very slightly lower than this for technical reasons.
>
> Cameras will generally have a maximum and minimum frame rate that they support. If you ask for a faster or slower frame rate, this will be *clamped* to the maximum or minimum that is achievable. These limits normally depend on the camera and the *camera mode*, the subject of Chapter 6, *Understanding Camera Modes*.

Controlling the Camera's White Balance

Setting the camera's white balance is another traditional camera function, even though it is actually a function of the software that drives the camera, and not of the image sensor itself (as was the case with exposure, for example). You can see how an image without a custom white balance mode (**Figure** 5-3) compares to one with a white balance mode specified (**Figure** 5-4).

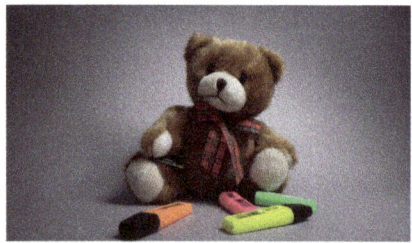

Figure 5-3
An image captured without a custom white balance mode

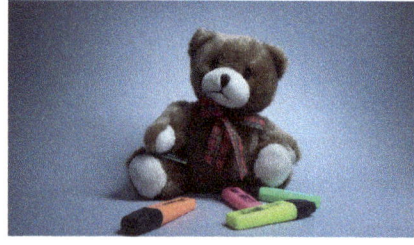

Figure 5-4
An image captured using the tungsten white balance mode

Choosing the White Balance Mode

By default, the camera system uses the "auto" white balance mode, which attempts to compensate for a very wide range of illuminants, ranging from very orange indoor lighting to very blue outdoor illumination. But you have a number of different modes that you can choose which work by constraining this range. We have:

`auto`
> Assume the illuminant may come from a very wide range of everyday sources (the default setting).

`incandescent`
> Assume the illuminant is some form of incandescent lighting.

`tungsten`
> Assume the illumination is provided by a tungsten filament.

`fluorescent`
> Assume the illuminant is some form of fluorescent light.

`indoor`
> Assume the camera is pointing at a scene with indoor lighting.

`daylight`
> Assume the scene is outdoor with daylight illumination.

`cloudy`
> Assume that the ambient conditions are a cloudy outdoor day.

You should set your choice with the `--awb` option, for example, to choose the daylight white-balance mode, use:

`rpicam-still --awb daylight -o daylight.jpg`

Setting Explicit Colour Gains

The AWB algorithm is really just choosing the red and blue gains that will be applied to the image to correct the colours. If you wish, you can set these values explicitly, though you will need to explore different settings to determine what values will be appropriate.

For example, to set a red gain of 1.5 and a blue gain of 2.0, you can use:

```
rpicam-still --awbgains 1.5,2.0 -o image.jpg
```

The gain values are given as red followed by blue and should be separated just by a comma (and no spaces).

In general, you can expect that the values you need to use will vary between different models of camera (for example, values that give a "correct" image for a camera module v2 will give an image with a very pronounced colour cast with an HQ cam).

Autofocus and Lens Position

Autofocus and a controllable lens are only available with the Camera Module 3. Other Raspberry Pi cameras, other than the v1 camera module, have lenses that can be controlled manually or (in the case of the v2 camera module) with a small tool that was supplied with the camera. This section only applies to the Camera Module 3.

Setting the Lens Position

The lens position can be set explicitly using the `--lens-position` parameter. The units are *dioptres*, which is a reciprocal distance measure calculated by:

```
lens_position = 1 / focal_distance_in_metres
```

For example, to focus on an object 2 metres away, set the lens position to 1 / 2 = 0.5.

By convention, the value zero is taken to mean "at infinity". Note that the relationship between the lens position and the focal distance is only approximate. There is variation between different camera modules, variation with temperature, and it will also change significantly if the lens is pointed up or down.

For example, to capture a still image focused at 10 metres away, please use:

```
rpicam-still --lens-position 0.1 -o 10m.jpg
```

The lens is moved immediately to position 0.1, after which it will not move again.

Setting the Autofocus Mode

The autofocus algorithm has three distinct modes.

manual

The autofocus algorithm is disabled and the lens position must be set manually using the `--lens-position` parameter, after which it will not move again.

auto

The camera performs an autofocus sweep when it camera starts, after which the lens does not move again. If you add the additional parameter `--autofocus-on-capture` (with no arguments), then another sweep will be repeated just before any still image is captured.

continuous

The lens will be moved continuously to find the best focus position at all times.

Normally the autofocus algorithm defaults to continuous mode, unless:

▸ You specified the `--lens-position` parameter, in which case it will be in manual mode.

▸ You used the `--autofocus-on-capture` parameter, in which case it will use the auto mode.

Let's try some examples. To capture a video with continuous autofocus:

`rpicam-vid --autofocus-mode continuous -o autofocus.h264`

And to capture a still image with a second autofocus cycle just before the capture:

`rpicam-still --autofocus-on-capture -o autofocus.jpg`

Image Processing Controls

The final category of controls are ones that affect how we render the image from the image sensor. For example, do we want to make it more colourful, sharper, or brighter?

Brightness

Image brightness can be changed with the `--brightness` parameter. It accepts a numeric value between `-1` and `1`, where `-1` means "black virtually everywhere" and `1` means "white virtually everywhere". The default value, meaning "normal brightness" is zero.

The brightness control works by adding a fixed positive (brighter) or negative (darker) value to all pixels.

Brightening an image a lot can lead to them looking a little washed out, conversely darkening them a lot can crush the dark areas of an image. Often the `--ev` parameter gives a better result than `--brightness`.

Example:

```
rpicam-hello --brightness 0.2
```

Contrast

Image contrast can be changed with the `--contrast` parameter. It accepts a numeric value from 0 upwards, where 0 means "no contrast at all" (the image will be grey almost everywhere) and 1 is the default meaning "normal contrast". Larger values produce more contrast in direct proportion.

The contrast control works by applying a gain (which is in fact the contrast parameter) to the difference between every pixel and the value of a grey pixel.

For an image with 20% more contrast, you could use:

```
rpicam-hello --contrast 1.2
```

Colour Saturation

Change colour saturation with the `--saturation` parameter. It accepts a numeric value from `0` upwards, where `0` means "no colour saturation at all" (the image will be greyscale) and `1` is the default meaning "normal colour saturation". Larger values produce more colour saturation in direct proportion.

If you wanted only 90% of the standard colour saturation, you could use:

```
rpicam-hello --saturation 0.9
```

Sharpness

You can change image sharpness with the `--sharpness` parameter. It accepts a numeric value from **0** upwards, where **0** means "no sharpening at all" (resulting in a soft image) and **1** is the default meaning "normal sharpening". Larger values produce more sharpening in direct proportion.

If you wanted only 50% more sharpening, you could use:

`rpicam-hello --sharpness 1.5`

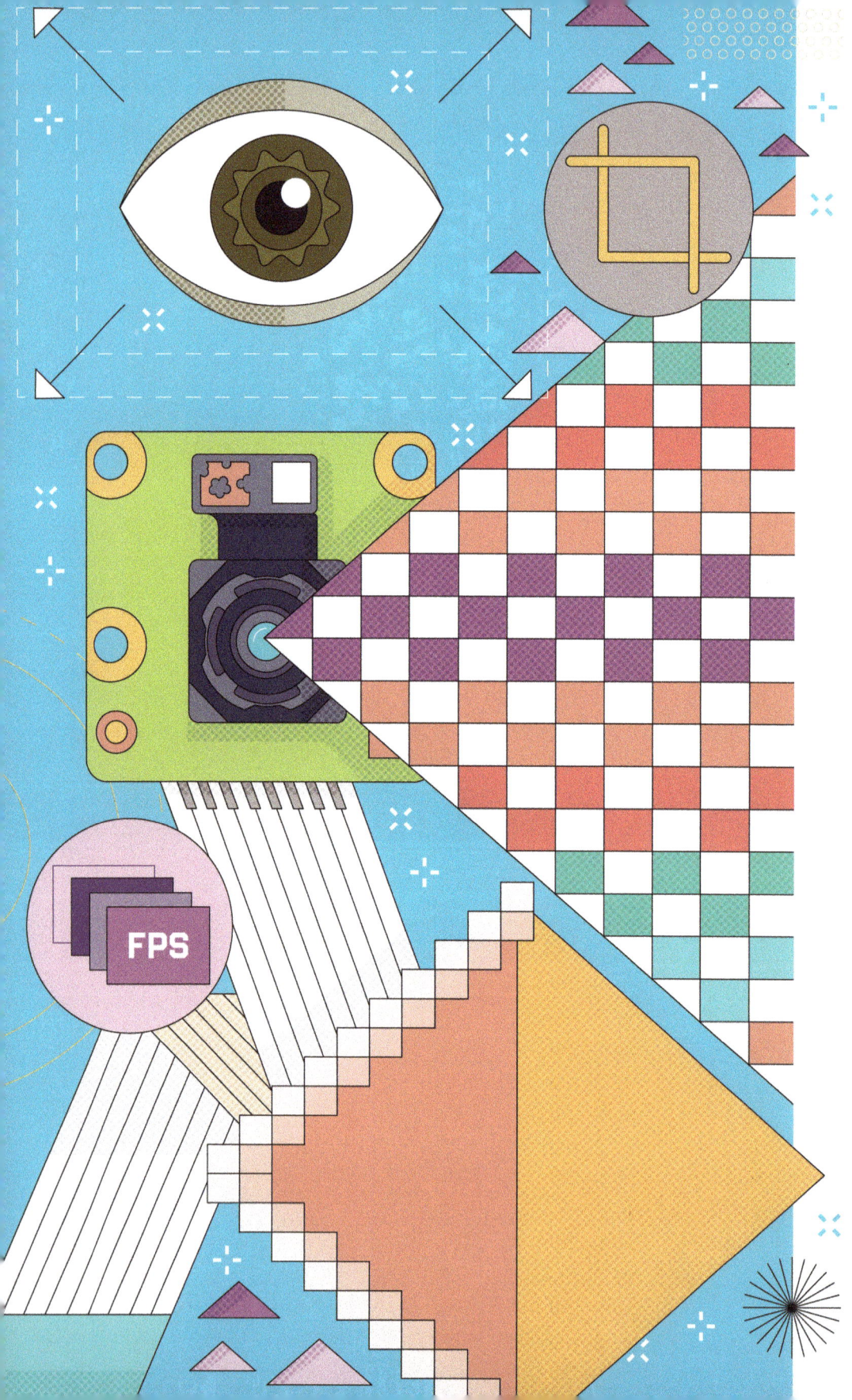

Chapter 6

Understanding Camera Modes

Choosing different camera modes

Cameras deliver sequences of images, and you can control certain aspects of how those images are delivered, like the exposure time or framerate. However, the limits of these parameters are all governed by the *mode* that the camera is operating in. For example, the current camera mode may have a maximum framerate that it will allow, and therefore any attempt to ask for a higher framerate will fail unless a new camera mode is selected beforehand.

Selecting a new camera mode is a relatively resource-intensive operation. It requires reprogramming much of the sensor's internal configuration, and therefore cannot happen while the camera is running, and delivering images. Instead, the camera must be stopped completely, reconfigured into the chosen mode, and finally restarted. This whole process can easily take several hundreds of milliseconds. Not a big deal in human timescales, but still, you'd notice a pause like that in a video recording.

Finally, the range of camera modes that is available is determined by the driver for the image sensor. To all intents and purposes this list of modes is fixed. Adding new modes is a quite technical procedure that will require detailed knowledge of the internals of the image sensor (probably from the manufacturer) and also of Linux kernel programming.

What does the Camera Mode affect?

The camera mode has an impact on a variety of fundamental characteristics of the image capture process. Let's look at the most significant of these.

Image Resolution

A sensor has a *native resolution*, which corresponds to the maximum image resolution that the sensor can provide. However, you can usually configure the sensor to output images of different sizes, as you'll see next.

Cropping

Instead of reading out the sensor's full array of pixels, giving you the native resolution, you can normally configure a sensor to read out only a window, or *crop*, from within the entire array of pixels. This limits the field of view — you don't get the full image that the sensor could have delivered — but in return, you may be able to read the image out more quickly, giving a higher maximum framerate.

When we describe the crop associated with a camera mode, we measure it in units of the full native sensor resolution, just as with other operations that affect the image resolution, such as *binning*.

Binning

Many sensors have a feature where each 2×2 block of pixels is averaged to create a single output pixel; this process is known as *binning*. The end result is an image with half the height and half the width of the full sensor resolution.

Binned modes produce images with lower noise (because of the averaging), but they are also — as with cropping — able to run at significantly higher framerates. Binned modes also give applications the possibility to deal with fewer pixels in every image, which is often helpful in preview or video use cases.

Very similar to binning is *skipping*. This too, turns blocks of 2×2 pixels into a single output pixel, though it does so simply by dropping three of them. Therefore, it doesn't benefit from the decreased noise levels.

The process of turning 2×2 pixel blocks into a single output pixel is referred to as *2×2 binning*. Although less common, some sensors may even support 4x4 binning modes, or modes that involve both 2×2 binning and 2×2 skipping.

Sensors normally also allow both cropping and binning.

Bit Depth

The camera mode also determines the number of bits in every pixel that it reads out. Although the output images from the camera system normally use 8-bit pixels, the values that come from the image sensor are normally larger, with typically 10 or 12 bits. Again, the sensor will normally have a native bit depth, although a camera mode may allow you to read out fewer. Here too, the benefit would be in achieving slightly higher framerates.

Other Special Modes

Beyond this, certain cameras may have special modes that support less common or particularly advanced features. One such example is the Camera Module 3, which has a special High Dynamic Range (HDR) mode that merges multiple pixels together to create an HDR image.

Finding out the available Modes

The easiest way to find out what camera modes are available is to type:

`rpicam-hello --list-cameras`

This will list the cameras attached to the system (usually just one), and for each it will list the available camera modes. For the HQ camera, for example, it will return the following (reformatted slightly for readability):

```
0:imx477 [4056x3040 12-bit RGGB](/base/soc/i2c0mux/i2c@1/imx477...
Modes:SRGGB10_CSI2P: 1332x990[120.05fps-(696,528)/2664x1980 crop]
      SRGGB12_CSI2P: 2028x1080[50.03fps-(0,440)/4056x2160 crop]
                     2028x1520[40.01fps-(0,0)/4056x3040 crop]
                     4056x3040[10.00fps-(0,0)/4056x3040 crop]
```

We can interpret this as follows:

Line 1:

There is just a single camera, numbered as camera **0**. This line also identifies it as an **IMX477** (the sensor in the HQ camera), with a native resolution of 4056×3040 pixels, and a native pixel depth of 12 bits.

Line 2:

This tells us there is just one **SRGGB10_CSI2P** mode (the *pixel format*). The number 10 in the name tells us that this is a 10-bit mode, rather than the more usual 12-bit modes below. It's clear this has been chosen to give us a maximum of just over 120 frames per second.

At the end of each line, we have the crop for that mode. This is given in the form **(x_offset, y_offset)/width x height**. So, this mode reads a 2664×1980 rectangle out of the native 4056×3040 image but *offset* with its top left corner at (696, 528) in the native image. A quick calculation (**4056 = 2 * 696 + 2664**) confirms that we're reading out the central portion of the image (and the same again in the vertical axis), as shown in **Figure 6-1**. Note how this camera mode involves both cropping (due to the offset) and binning (2x2 binning, to be specific, because the 2664×1980 rectangle is exactly twice the output image size).

After the pixel format, every mode lists the output resolution for that camera mode. If you ask your camera application for images larger than this, while using this mode, then it will upscale them.

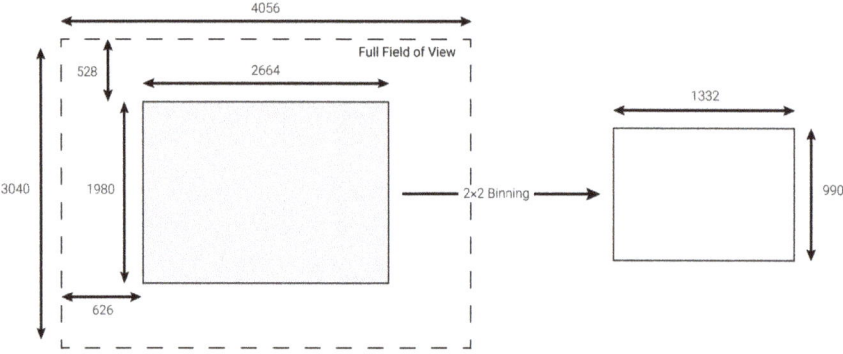

Figure 6-1 Cropping and binning

Lines 3–5:

Next, we have three **SRGGB12_CSI2P** or 12 bit modes, with framerates ranging from about 50fps down to about 10fps for the full resolution version. When the two crop offsets (**x_offset** and **y_offset** above) are both zero (as in the case of the last two modes), then this is a full field of view mode.

 Note also how the 2028×1080 mode is very similar to the 2028×1520 mode — same width, both using 2×2 binning — but the slightly shorter image height allows a higher framerate. It's clearly intended to allow applications to record 1080p50 videos.

Which mode to use?

This is a surprisingly difficult question. Different camera modes have different features and advantages, and there's no one-size-fits-all method to decide which mode to use based on, for example, the final output image size that an application has requested.

For instance, is the application happy to accept some upscaling? Or would it rather use the highest resolution camera modes, and downscale the image, to get better image quality?

Does an application prioritise getting the widest possible field of view from the image sensor, or would it be happy to sacrifice the field of view in return for faster framerates?

Whilst `rpicam-apps` will attempt to make a reasonable choice for you based on the arguments provided, it won't always be right. For this reason, it's possible for the user to override this selection process and choose exactly which camera mode to use.

Selecting a Camera Mode explicitly

`rpicam-apps` have a number of mode related command line parameters that allow you to select exactly which camera mode you want to use. They all take a mode of the form `width:height:bitdepth:packing` where:

width
> The output width of the camera mode

height
> The output height of the camera mode

bitdepth
> The bit depth of the camera mode

packing
> The letter **P** (*packed*) or **U** (*unpacked*)

Packed formats will be preferable for most people as they use less memory bandwidth and are therefore more efficient, though users who want access to the raw pixel data from the sensor (beyond the scope of this guide) may prefer unpacked formats.

The command line parameters are named as follows, where `mode` is of the form `width:height:bitdepth:packing`:

- `rpicam-hello` accepts the parameter `--viewfinder-mode mode`.
- `rpicam-vid` accepts the parameter `--mode mode`.

> **rpicam-still** accepts both the parameters `--viewfinder-mode mode` which defines the camera mode for the preview, and `--mode mode` which defines the camera mode for the actual still image capture.

For example, using an HQ camera:

`rpicam-vid -o 1080p50.h264 --mode 2028:1080:12:P --framerate 50`

... will record a 1080p resolution at 50fps. We know it can reach this framerate because we have explicitly chosen a camera mode that is capable of this. The camera mode, outputting a larger image than 1920×1080, also guarantees that no upscaling is happening.

Raw Images and Camera Tuning

We've mentioned how camera modes define the resolution and format of the *raw pixels* that are read from the camera's image sensor. But what exactly are these raw pixels?

The pixels that we obtain from the sensor require a large amount of processing to turn them into viewable images. For a start, each pixel records only one colour — red, green, or blue — instead of all three. This kind of image is often referred to as a *Bayer image*, shown in **Figure 6-2**, named after Bryce Bayer who pioneered their use at Kodak. Although other forms of image sensor exist, so-called Bayer sensors remain very popular because they work well and are cost-effective.

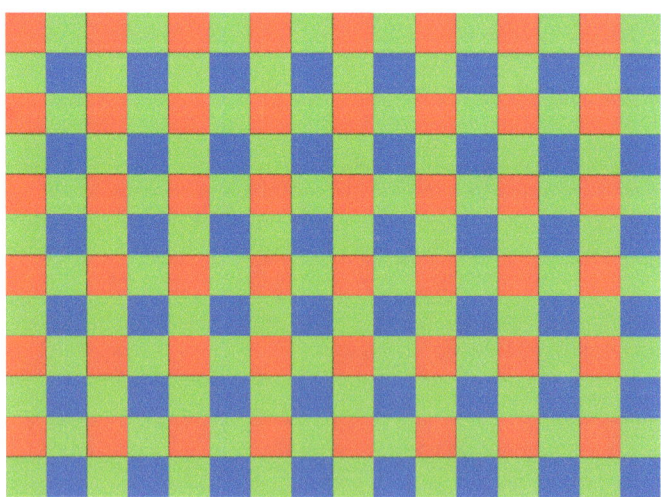

Figure 6-2 A Bayer pattern — every pixel is only red, green, or blue

You're also now in a position to understand why the IMX477 was described by `rpicam-hello --list-cameras` as an RGGB sensor. It's because it's made up of pairs of rows where every Red-Green pixel row is followed by a Green-Blue row.

Not only do the 'missing' colours have to be calculated (or interpolated), but a whole host of other corrections have to be applied. This includes fixing any 'stuck' pixels, reducing noise levels, and making the brightness levels and colours look correct. Finally, the image needs to be delivered in the correct resolution and format to the end user or application.

Most of the time, all we want is the fully processed final image that comes out of the camera system, but there are certainly applications — sometimes scientific in nature, or for professional photographers — where access to the raw sensor data can be useful.

You can even capture the raw sensor data in a DNG file (Adobe's *Digital NeGative* format). For example:

`rpicam-still --raw -o image.jpg`

will save the raw file **image.dng** alongside the requested JPEG file **image.jpg**. You would need special software tools to use or convert these DNG files, which lie beyond the scope of this guide.

Tuning Files

Finally, it's worth noting that you have many choices in how you turn the raw image into a final picture. Raspberry Pi provides a default *tuning file* which supplies the various parameters that control this process, and you can look at them in the file **imx477.json**, which should be available on the Pi's filesystem (usually in **/usr/share/libcamera/ipa/rpi/vc4**). This is a JSON-formatted text file for the IMX477 sensor (in the HQ camera) with each named block of parameters controlling one specific aspect of the process.

Raspberry Pi 5 computers have tuning files that contain different parameters from the tuning files for all earlier Raspberry Pi devices. The Raspberry Pi 5 versions can be found in **/usr/share/libcamera/ipa/rpi/pisp** instead.

If the default camera tuning does not suit your application, we encourage you to develop your own camera tuning files, and to consider contributing them back to the wider Raspberry Pi user community. Help and documentation are available for those who would like to get involved: **magpi.cc/camdocs**.

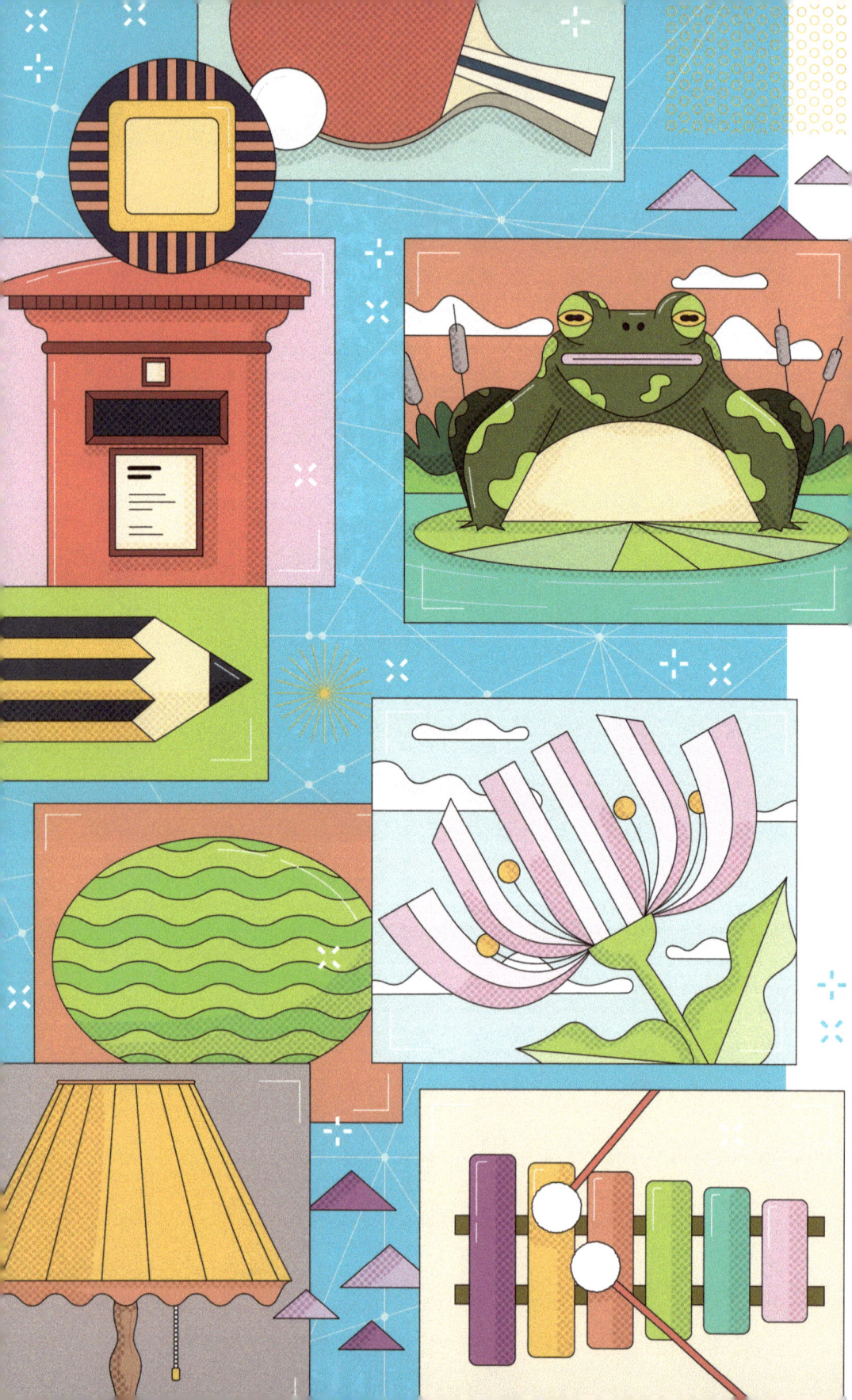

Chapter 7

Get started with Raspberry Pi AI Kit

Add neural processing to your camera

The Raspberry Pi AI Kit bundles the Raspberry Pi M.2 HAT+ with a Hailo AI acceleration module you can use with Raspberry Pi 5. The kit contains the Hailo AI module containing a neural processing unit (NPU), a Raspberry Pi M.2 HAT+, to connect the AI module to your Raspberry Pi 5, a thermal pad pre-fitted between the module and the M.2 HAT+, a mounting hardware kit, and a 16mm stacking GPIO header as shown in **Figure 7-1**.

The AI module features a 13 tera-operations per second (TOPS) neural network inference accelerator built around the Hailo-8L chip in an M.2 2242 form factor.

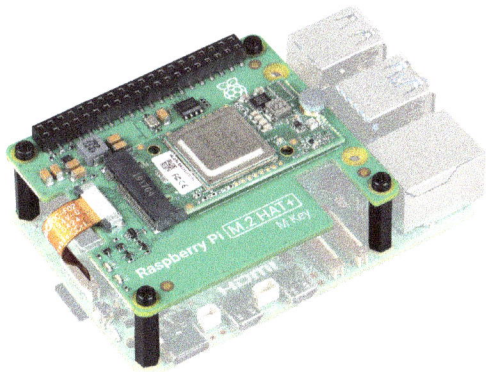

Figure 7-1 AI Kit attached to Raspberry Pi 5

To use the AI Kit, you will need a Raspberry Pi 5. Each AI Kit comes with a pre-installed AI module, ribbon cable, GPIO stacking header, and mounting hardware. Complete the following instructions to install your AI Kit:

First, ensure that your Raspberry Pi runs the latest software. Run the following commands to update:

`sudo apt update && sudo apt full-upgrade`

Next, ensure that your Raspberry Pi firmware is sufficiently new. Run this command to see what firmware you're running:

`sudo rpi-eeprom-update`

If you see 6 December 2023 or a later date, proceed to the next step. If you see a date earlier than 6 December 2023, run the following command to open the Raspberry Pi Configuration CLI:

`sudo raspi-config`

Click **Advanced Options**, then select **Bootloader Version** and choose **Latest**. Then, exit `raspi-config` with **Finish** or the **ESC** key.

Run this command to update your firmware to the latest version:

`sudo rpi-eeprom-update -a`

Then, reboot with `sudo reboot`. See **magpi.cc/updatebootloader** for more details on updating your firmware image.

Installing the AI Kit

Disconnect the power first!

Always disconnect your Raspberry Pi from power before connecting or disconnecting a device from the M.2 slot. See **magpi.cc/power** for more details.

Disconnect the Raspberry Pi from power before beginning installation. For the best performance, we recommend using the AI Kit with the Raspberry Pi Active Cooler. If you have an Active Cooler, install it (see **Figure 7-2**) before installing the AI Kit.

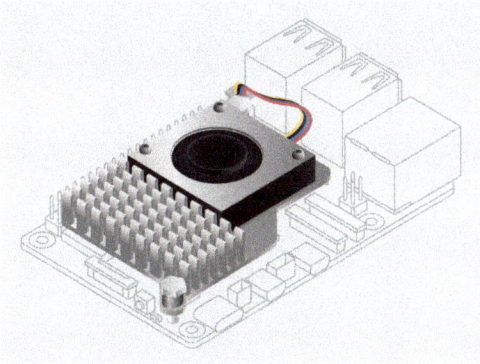

Figure 7-2 Attaching Raspberry Pi's Active Cooler

Install the spacers using four of the provided screws. Firmly press the GPIO stacking header on top of the Raspberry Pi GPIO pins; orientation does not matter as long as all pins fit into place. Disconnect the ribbon cable from the AI Kit and insert the other end into the PCIe port of your Raspberry Pi. Lift the ribbon cable holder from both sides, then insert the cable with the copper contact points facing inward, towards the USB ports. With the ribbon cable fully and evenly inserted into the PCIe port, push the cable holder down from both sides to secure the ribbon cable firmly in place.

Set the AI Kit on top of the spacers and use the four remaining screws to secure it in place.

Insert the ribbon cable into the slot on the AI Kit. Lift the ribbon cable holder from both sides, then insert the cable with the copper contact points facing up. With the ribbon cable fully and evenly inserted into the port, push the cable holder down from both sides to secure the ribbon cable firmly in place as shown in **Figure 7-3**.

Congratulations, you have successfully installed the AI Kit (**Figure 7-4**). Connect your Raspberry Pi to power; Raspberry Pi OS will automatically detect the AI Kit.

Getting started

This section will help you set up the Raspberry Pi AI Kit with your Raspberry Pi 5. This will enable you to run **rpicam-apps** camera demos using the Hailo AI neural network accelerator.

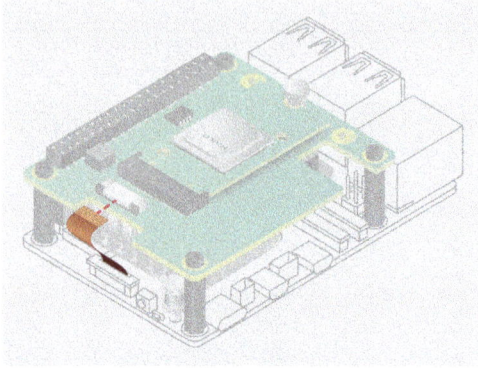

Figure 7-3 Inserting the ribbon cable

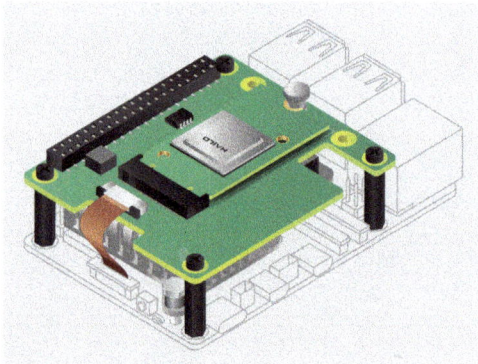

Figure 7-4 The completed AI Kit and Raspberry Pi 5

Attach the camera to your Raspberry Pi 5 board (see "Connecting and testing your camera" on page 10). You can skip reconnecting your Raspberry Pi to power, because you'll need to disconnect your Raspberry Pi from power for the next step.

Follow the instructions to enable PCIe Gen 3.0 (see **magpi.cc/pcigen3** for complete details). This step is optional, but highly recommended to achieve the best performance with your AI Kit.

```
sudo raspi-config
```

Complete the following steps to enable PCIe Gen 3.0 speeds:

1. Select **Advanced Options** from the menu.
2. Select **PCIe Speed**, then Choose **Yes** to enable PCIe Gen 3 mode.
3. Select **Finish** to exit and choose **Yes** when asked "Would you like to reboot now?".

Install the dependencies required to use the AI Kit. Run the following command from a terminal window:

`sudo apt install hailo-all`

This installs the following dependencies:

- Hailo kernel device driver and firmware
- HailoRT middleware software
- Hailo Tappas core post-processing libraries
- The rpicam-apps Hailo post-processing software demo stages

To make these settings take effect, reboot your Raspberry Pi with `sudo reboot`. To confirm that everything is installed correctly, run the following command:

`hailortcli fw-control identify`

If you see output similar to the following, you've successfully installed the AI Kit and its software dependencies:

```
Executing on device: 0000:01:00.0
Identifying board
Control Protocol Version: 2
Firmware Version: 4.17.0 (release,app,extended context switch b...
Logger Version: 0
Board Name: Hailo-8
Device Architecture: HAILO8L
Serial Number: HLDDLBB234500054
Part Number: HM21LB1C2LAE
Product Name: HAILO-8L AI ACC M.2 B+M KEY MODULE EXT TMP
```

Additionally, you can run `dmesg | grep -i hailo` to check the kernel logs, which should yield output similar to the following:

```
[3.04] hailo: Init module. driver version 4.17.0
...
[3.23] hailo 00:01:00.0: Probing: Added board 1e60-2864,/dev/hailo0
```

To ensure the camera is operating correctly, run the following command:

```
rpicam-hello -t 10s
```

This starts the camera and shows a preview window for ten seconds. Once you have verified everything is installed correctly, it's time to run some demos.

Run the demos

The rpicam-apps suite of camera applications implements a post-processing framework (**magpi.cc/postproc**). This section contains a few demo post-processing stages that highlight some of the capabilities of the AI Kit.

The following demos use **rpicam-hello**, which by default displays a preview window. However, you can use other **rpicam-apps** instead, including **rpicam-vid** and **rpicam-still**. You may need to add or modify some command line options to make the demo commands compatible with other applications.

To begin, download the post-processing JSON files required for the demos. These files determine which post-processing stages to run and configure the behaviour of each stage. For example, you can enable, disable, strengthen, or weaken the temporal filtering in the object detection demos. Or you could enable or disable the output mask drawing in the segmentation demo.

To download the entire collection of post-processing JSON files, clone the **rpicam-apps** repo. Run the following command to clone only the most recent commit from the repo, which uses less storage space on your Raspberry Pi:

```
git clone --depth 1 \
    https://github.com/raspberrypi/rpicam-apps.git ~/rpicam-apps
```

Object Detection

This demo, shown in **Figure 7-5**, displays bounding boxes around objects detected by a neural network. To disable the viewfinder, use the **-n** flag. To return purely textual output describing the objects detected, add the **-v 2** option. Run the following command to try the demo on your Raspberry Pi:

```
rpicam-hello -t 0 --post-process-file \
    ~/rpicam-apps/assets/hailo_yolov6_inference.json \
    --lores-width 640 --lores-height 640
```

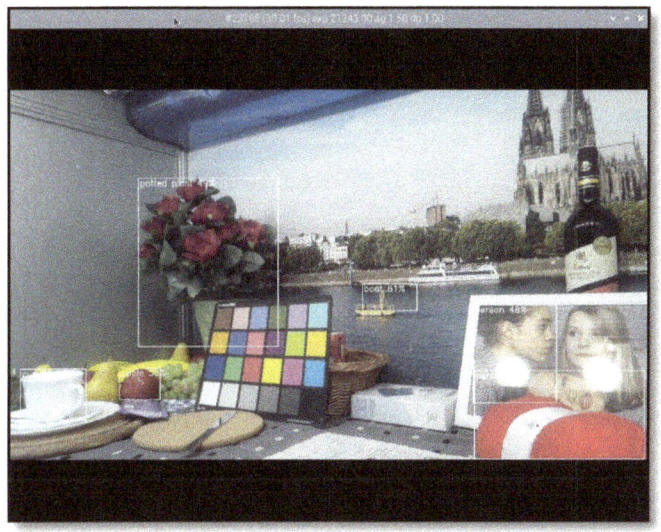

Figure 7-5   Object detection in Raspberry Pi OS

You can try another model with different trade-offs in performance and efficiency. To run the demo with the Yolov8 model, run the following command:

```
rpicam-hello -t 0 --post-process-file \
  ~/rpicam-apps/assets/hailo_yolov8_inference.json \
  --lores-width 640 --lores-height 640
```

To run the demo with the YoloX model, run the following command:

```
rpicam-hello -t 0 --post-process-file \
  ~/rpicam-apps/assets/hailo_yolox_inference.json \
  --lores-width 640 --lores-height 640
```

To run the demo with the Yolov5 Person and Face model:

```
rpicam-hello -t 0 --post-process-file \
  ~/rpicam-apps/assets/hailo_yolov5_personface.json \
  --lores-width 640 --lores-height 640
```

Image Segmentation

This demo performs object detection and segments the object by drawing a colour mask on the viewfinder image. Run the following command to try the demo on your Raspberry Pi:

```
rpicam-hello -t 0 --post-process-file \
  ~/rpicam-apps/assets/hailo_yolov5_segmentation.json \
  --lores-width 640 --lores-height 640 --framerate 20
```

Pose Estimation

This demo performs 17-point human pose estimation, drawing lines connecting the detected points. Run the following command to try the demo on your Raspberry Pi:

```
rpicam-hello -t 0 --post-process-file \
  ~/rpicam-apps/assets/hailo_yolov8_pose.json \
  --lores-width 640 --lores-height 640
```

Hailo has also created a set of demos that you can run on a Raspberry Pi 5, available in the **hailo-rpi5-examples** GitHub repository (**magpi.cc/hailorpi5**).

You can find Hailo's extensive model zoo, which contains a large number of neural networks, in the **hailo_model_zoo** repository (**magpi.cc/hailozoo**).

Visit the Hailo community forums and developer zone (**community.hailo.ai**) for further discussions on the Hailo hardware and tooling.

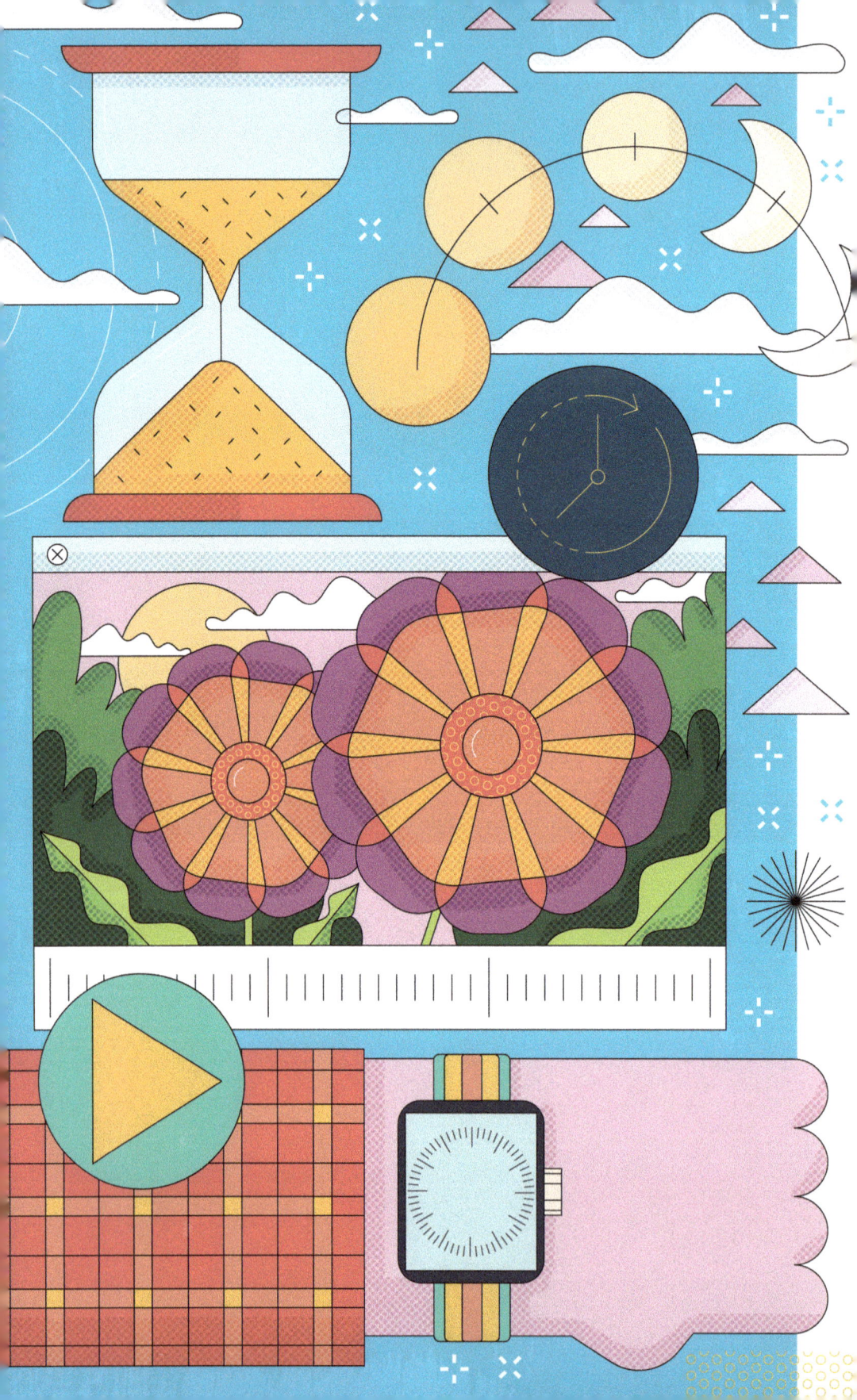

Chapter 8

Time-lapse photography

Make a device to capture photographs at regular intervals, then turn these images into a video

Time-lapse photography reveals exciting things about the world which you wouldn't otherwise be able see. These are things that happen too slowly for us to perceive: bread rising and plants growing (as in **Figure 8-1**); the clouds, sun, moon, and stars crossing the sky; shadows moving across the land. In this chapter, we'll be making a Raspberry Pi-based device that lets you watch things that are too slow to observe with the naked eye. To do this, we will capture lots of still photographs and combine these frames into a video.

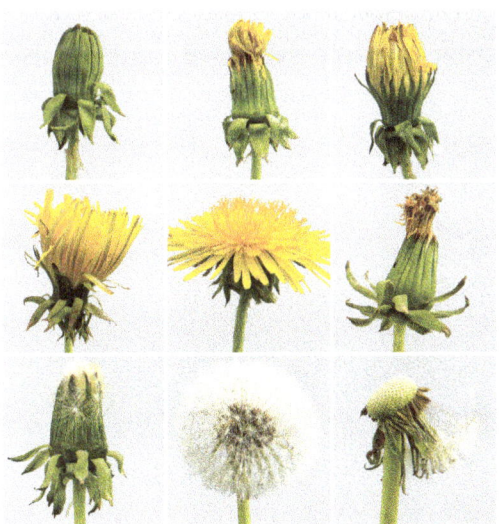

Figure 8-1 Time-lapse photography is ideal for capturing lengthy natural processes

Connect and test the camera

First, with Raspberry Pi turned off, make sure your camera is connected, enabled, and tested as described in "Connecting and testing your camera" on page 10. You can test the camera by running the following:

`rpicam-hello`

This will open a camera preview window and display the camera image there for about five seconds.

Launch a web server

If you want to access your captured images remotely, you can launch a web server from wherever you save the images. Using the Raspberry menu, open the Accessories category and click Terminal. Create a folder in your home directory and change to that directory:

```
mkdir ~/camera-timelapse
cd ~/camera-timelapse
```

Next, use Python's **http.server** module to launch a web server:

`python3 -m http.server`

Python will tell you what port it's listening on (8000 by default) but won't tell you the IP address:

`Serving HTTP on 0.0.0.0 port 8000 (http://0.0.0.0:8000/) ...`

Go to another computer, open a browser, and visit your web server using a URL like **http://hostname:8000** (where **hostname** is your Raspberry Pi's hostname). If that doesn't work, you can use its IP address and port, such as **http://192.168.1.45:8000**. To determine its IP address, open a new Terminal window on your Raspberry Pi and run **hostname -I**.

Once you have the page loaded, you should see an empty directory listing in the web browser.

Back on your Raspberry Pi, leave the web server running and open a second Terminal window, then change to the directory you created earlier:

`cd ~/camera-timelapse`

Run the following command, and on the other computer, refresh the browser page. You should see the image file listed.

`rpicam-still -o testimage.jpg`

Click the image name and you'll see the image in your browser as shown in **Figure 8-2**. You can stop the web server by switching to the Terminal window where you launched it and pressing **CTRL+C**. But keep it running for now, because you can use the web server as an easy way to transfer files.

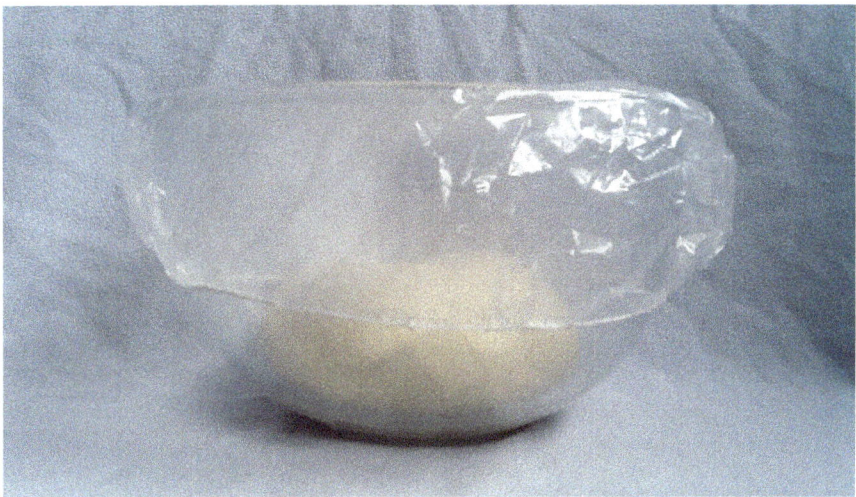

Figure 8-2 Some bread dough ready to prove. Watch it rise in your video.

Capture the images

Set up your scene and check the positioning of the camera:

`rpicam-still --width 1920 --height 1080 -o testimageFullHD.jpg`

The width and height have been changed to capture a smaller image in 16:9 aspect ratio. This makes things easier later. The top and bottom are cropped, so make sure that your subject is in frame. Run this to start the capture:

`rpicam-still --width 1920 --height 1080 -t 10800000 \`
`  --timelapse 10000 -o frame%04d.jpg`

This takes a photo every ten seconds for three hours. If you want to stop it sooner, switch back to the Terminal window where you ran this command, and press **CTRL+C**.

Prepare to make the video

You can render the video on Raspberry Pi, but — depending on the model — this can take a long time. So you may prefer to transfer the files to a more powerful computer instead. Whichever method you decide to use, you will need to install the tools on the rendering machine; for Raspberry Pi, as well as Debian- or Ubuntu-based Linux distributions, enter:

`sudo apt-get install ffmpeg`

This installs the FFmpeg tool which you'll use to convert images into a video. On a macOS system running Homebrew, run `brew install ffmpeg`.

To copy the images to a remote machine, you can download them from the web server using `wget` or `curl`. For example, this will download them into your current directory:

`wget -r -nd -A jpg http://hostname:8000`

Change the hostname and filename numbers accordingly. Or if you don't have `wget`, you can use `curl`, but this command will create files even when they aren't found on the server, so you will need to delete any *.jpg* files that contain HTML results indicating 404 HTTP errors.

`curl 'http://hostname:8000/frame[0001-0766].jpg' -O`

Make an Animated GIF

Instead of video, make an animated GIF with ImageMagick (`sudo apt install imagemagick`). For a GIF, you should use smaller images, captured less frequently.

`convert frame*.jpg anim.gif`

Make the video

The final step is to assemble the video. Run the following command to start the rendering process, which is shown in **Figure 8-3**:

`ffmpeg -i frame%04d.jpg -crf 4 -b:v 10M video.webm`

WebM is an open video format that can be displayed directly in most browsers. However, other video formats are available. When the rendering process has finished, you'll be able to view the video in a browser (or a video player such as VLC). The default frame rate is 25fps. This compresses three hours of images taken at ten-second intervals to about 40 seconds of video. You can adjust this with the **-framerate** command-line option. The bitrate (**-b**) has been set high, and the Constant Rate Factor (**-crf**) has been kept low, to produce a good-quality video.

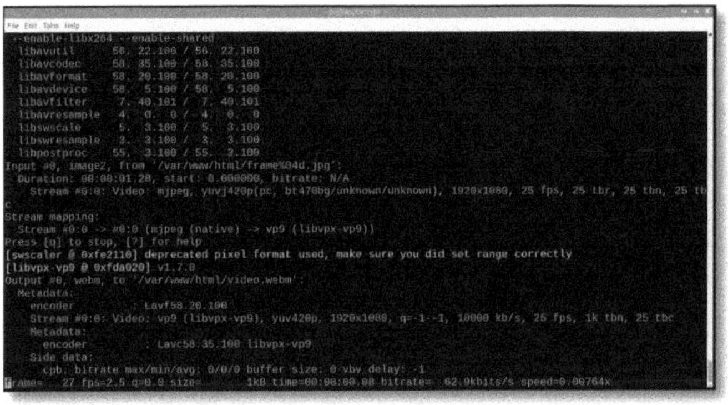

Figure 8-3 Running the rendering process on a Raspberry Pi

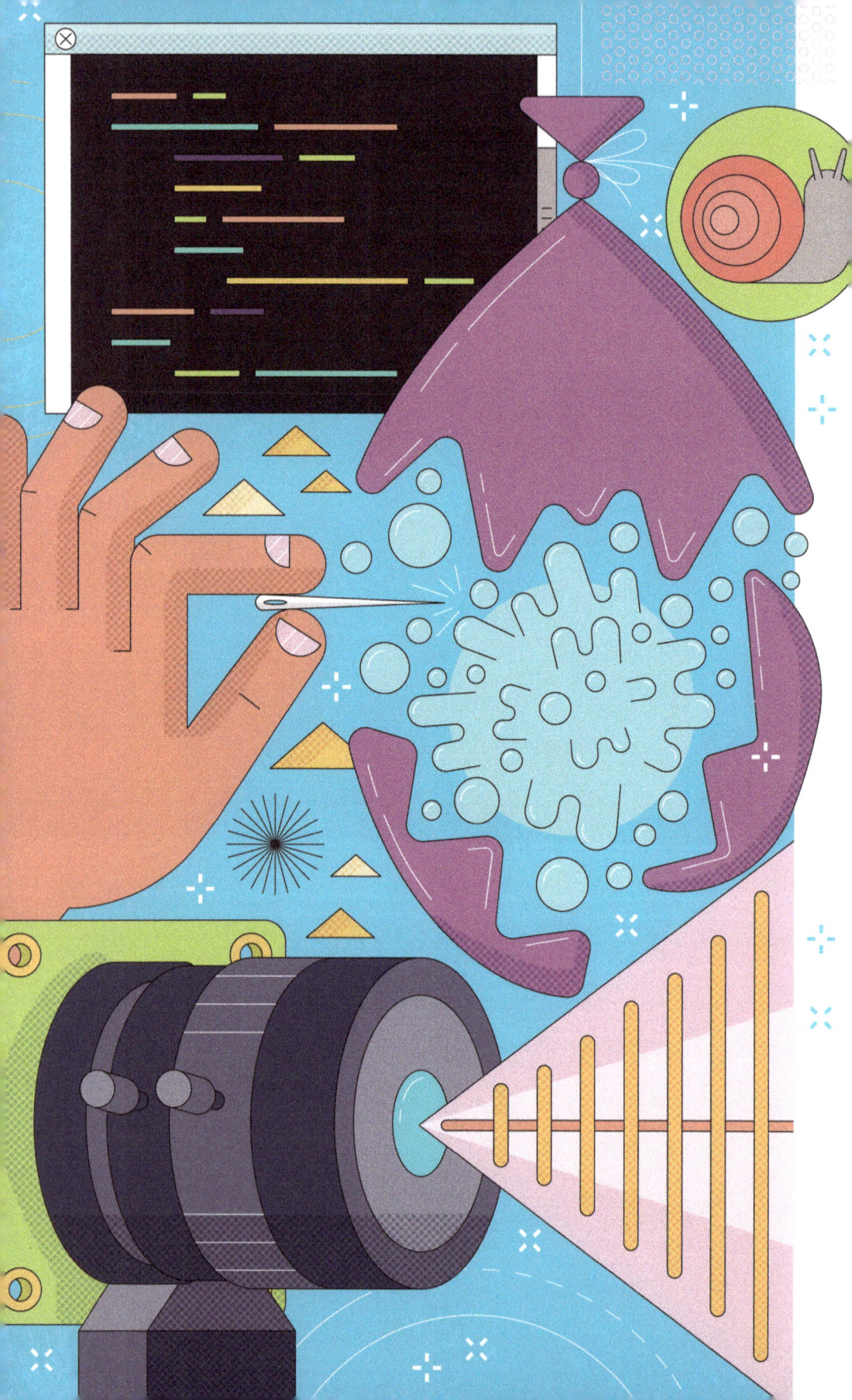

Chapter 9

High-speed photography

Make dazzling slow-motion clips of exciting events

At first glance it seems counter-intuitive, but in order to create a smooth slow-motion movie, you need a high-speed camera. Essentially, a movie is just a collection of still photos, or frames, all played one after the other at a speed that matches the original action. A slow-motion clip is produced by recording more frames than are normally needed and then playing them back at a reduced speed. Normal film is typically recorded at 24 frames per second (fps), with video frame rates varying between 25 and 29fps depending on which format/region is involved. So, if you record at 50fps and play back at 25fps, the action will appear to be taking place at half the original speed. It's actually a little more complicated than that with the use of *interlaced frames*, but you don't really need to consider them here.

Recording at a high frame rate

The original software for the Camera Module was limited in terms of the frame rates it could cope with, but a subsequent update added new functionality so that clips can now be recorded at up to 90fps (or 120fps on the HQ Camera). There is one slight limitation: high frame rates are achieved by combining pixels from the camera sensor, so you have to sacrifice resolution. Depending on your exact hardware setup, a high-speed mode of 90fps may be achieved most consistently at a lower resolution such as 640×480. This is still good enough to capture decent-quality images, though.

A quick way of getting started is to pick some everyday objects and record them in motion. How about a dropped egg hitting a table top? A pull-back toy car crashing through some Lego blocks? Or even the old favourite of a water balloon bursting? It's best to do the last one outside!

Set up for recording

Once you've chosen your subject, you'll need a way of holding and angling the camera, and some way of lighting the scene. Neither needs to be sophisticated: a normal desk lamp works fine for extra illumination indoors, while a 'helping-hand' work aid (or tripod) is brilliant for keeping the camera stable at tricky angles (see **Figure 9-1** and **Figure 9-2**). You might also want to invest in a longer cable for the camera. You can get a longer cable for less than £2.

> With Camera Module v1, its red LED will illuminate when you're recording, which can cause undesirable reflections. You can just block the LED with a blob of modelling clay or turn it off completely by adding the line `disable_camera_led=1` to your **/boot/firmware/config.txt** file. This isn't needed for a Camera Module v2 (or later) or HQ Camera.

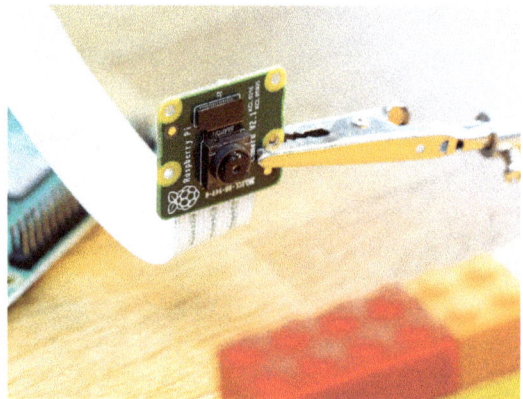

Figure 9-1   The high-speed camera setup

Fine-tune your video specifications

The command for capturing video with the Raspberry Pi camera is **rpicam-vid**, best run from a Terminal window. There are a number of command options that you can specify:

`--framerate`
Sets the frame rate.

`--width` and `-height`
Specifies the width and height of the frames.

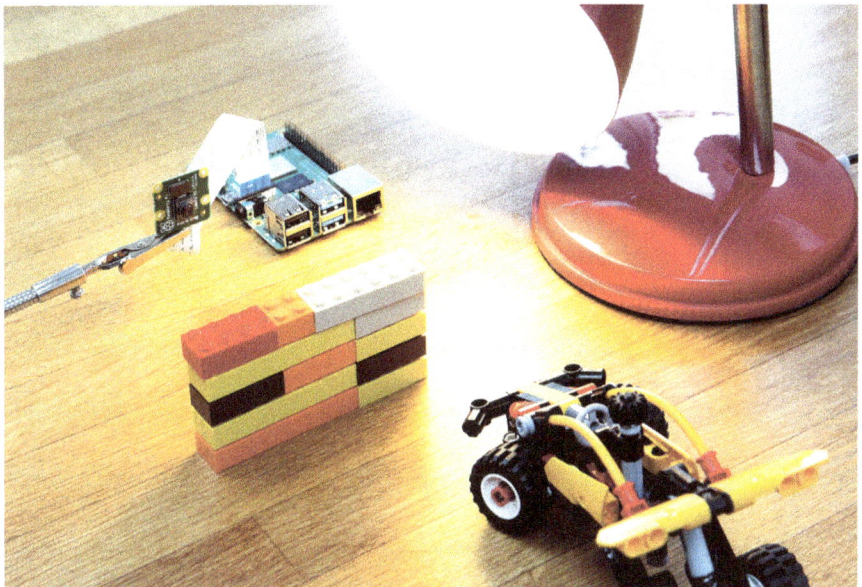

Figure 9-2 Another view of the setup

`-t`

Allows you to set how long to record for.

`-o`

Specifies the file name to use for the saved movie.

`-n`

Disables preview mode.

So, putting all of that together, the following commands would capture a five-second clip at 90fps and save the resulting movie (without sound) in the file **test.mp4**:

```
rpicam-vid -n --width 640 --height 480 --framerate 90 -t 5000 \
    --codec libav -o test.mp4
```

See "MP4 Files, Audio and other Container Formats" on page 31 for instructions on recording an MP4 with sound. Now that you've recorded your movie clip, you can play it with the free VLC player, which is preinstalled along with Raspberry Pi OS.

VLC has some handy features which can be accessed by clicking the **Advanced Controls** option from the **View** menu. These include the extremely useful **Frame by Frame** button that appears on the Advanced Controls just above the regular player controls. You can also alter the playback speed to slow things down even further.

To extend the project, how about connecting a break-beam IR sensor pair via the GPIO pins and using these to trigger the camera recording? The Python Picamera2 library (see Chapter 10, *Use Python with Picamera2*) provides full access to the camera's functions and could be used with your code.

Capturing the clip

Now that it's all set up, you're ready to capture the action.

Lights

Get your scene lined up and lit, then test how it looks by using the camera preview mode for five seconds:

```
rpicam-hello --width 640 --height 480
```

Camera

Type the command, ready for execution (but don't press **ENTER** yet):

```
rpicam-vid -n --width 640 --height 480 --framerate 90 -t 7000 \
    --codec libav -o myvid1.mp4
```

Once triggered, this will capture a seven-second clip.

Action

When everything is ready, hit **ENTER** and then release the car, drop the egg, or burst the balloon. You'll have footage before and after the event, which can be trimmed with some post-production editing.

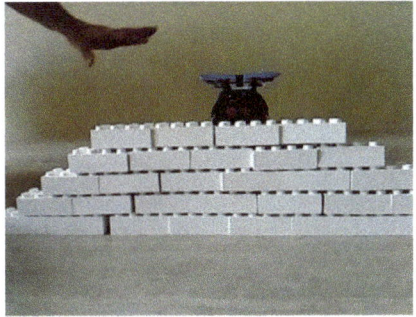

Figure 9-3
Bricks carefully stacked...

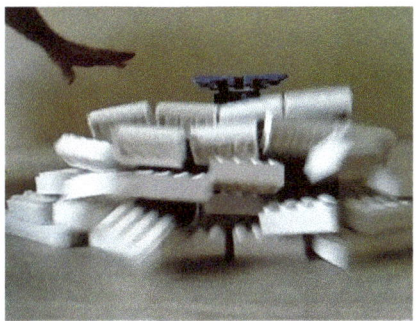

Figure 9-4
...soon take flight...

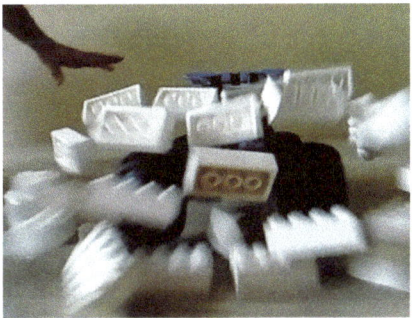

Figure 9-5
...when something comes...

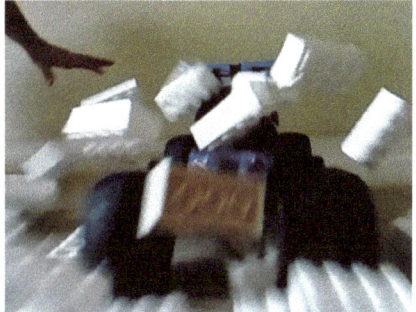

Figure 9-6
...bursting through!

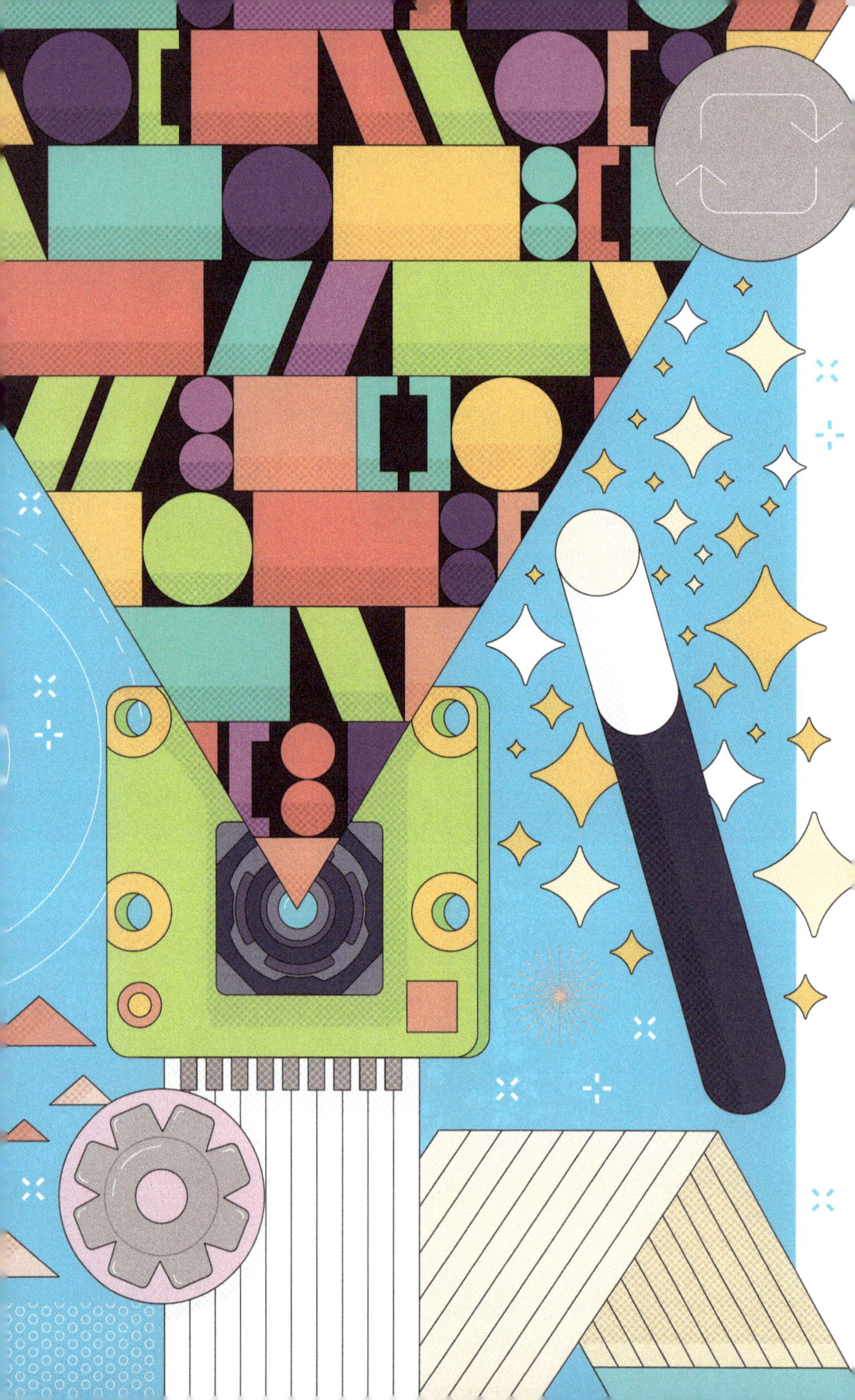

Chapter 10

Use Python with Picamera2

Control your camera with code

The Picamera2 library is a rpicam-based replacement for Picamera, which was a Python interface to Raspberry Pi's legacy camera stack. Picamera2 presents an easy-to-use Python API. Documentation about Picamera2 is available on GitHub (**magpi.cc/picam2git**) and in the Picamera2 manual (**magpi.cc/picam2man**).

Installation

Recent Raspberry Pi OS images include Picamera2 with all the GUI (Qt and OpenGL) dependencies. Recent Raspberry Pi OS Lite images include Picamera2 without the GUI dependencies, although you can display preview images outside of the desktop environment using DRM (Direct Rendering Manager).

If your Raspberry Pi OS image did not include Picamera2, run the following commands to install Picamera2 with all of the GUI dependencies:

```
sudo apt update
sudo apt install -y python3-picamera2
```

If you don't want the GUI dependencies, add **--no-install-recommends** to that command.

> **Use your distribution's version of Picamera2**
>
> If you previously installed Picamera2 with `pip`, uninstall it with: `pip3 uninstall picamera2`. This ensures you're using the Raspberry Pi-recommended version.

Testing Picamera2

Now that it's installed, let's try a simple example to make sure it's working. You can use your favourite text editor, or if you'd like to use an *Integrated Development Environment* (IDE), you can open up Thonny (click the Raspberry menu, then click the Programming category and select Thonny). Either way, save the file as **picam2_test.py**, and run it from the command line (`python picam2_test.py`) or from Thonny (click the run icon in the toolbar).

```python
import time
from picamera2 import Picamera2, Preview

cam = Picamera2()

preview_config = cam.create_preview_configuration()
cam.configure(preview_config)
cam.start_preview(Preview.QTGL)

cam.start()
time.sleep(5)
cam.stop()
cam.stop_preview()
```

The preview window will appear for 5 seconds and then close. If you need to run this from the console rather than the desktop environment, replace **Preview.QTGL** in **start_preview(Preview.QTGL)** with **Preview.DRM**. This will force the use of the Direct Rendering Manager. See "DRM Preview Window" on page 40 for more details.

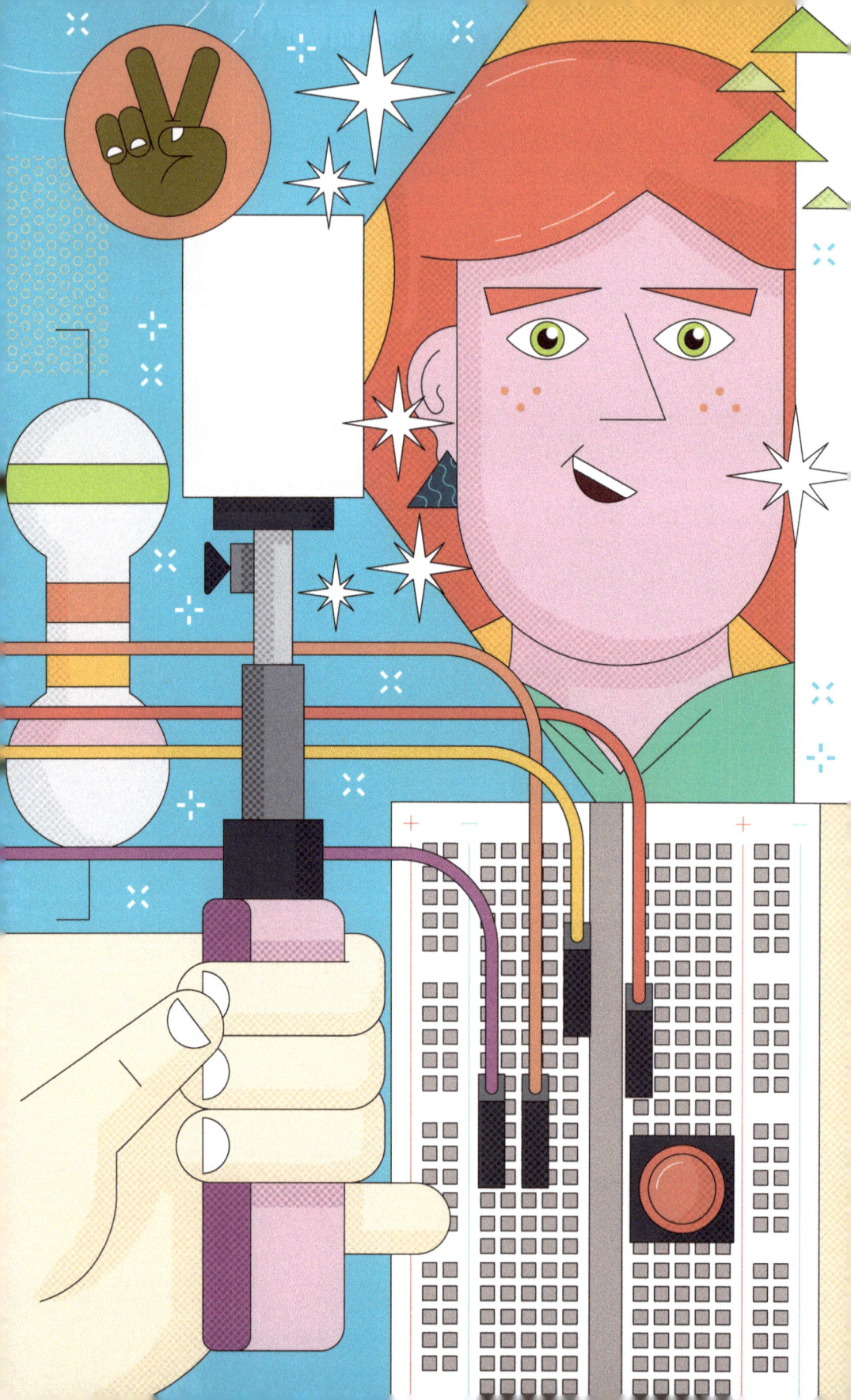

Chapter 11

Stop-motion and selfies

Wire up a physical push-button to take photos

Have you been reading the last few chapters and thinking you'd like to take a picture with a Raspberry Pi camera with less hassle? In this tutorial we'll show you how to take a photo with a click of a button, just like a real camera. This could be useful for many projects (for example, time-lapse photography), but in this chapter we are focusing on stop-motion animation. We also show how to create your own selfie stick!

What you'll need

- Camera Module / HQ Camera
- Push-button
- Breadboard (optional)
- Jumper wires
- Raspberry Pi case with a hole for the camera cable (selfie stick)
- Long wires (selfie stick)
- A stick, slim metal pole etc. (selfie stick)

Wire up the button

If you haven't already shut down your Raspberry Pi, do so now and unplug it from power. Next, connect the button to Raspberry Pi via a jumper wire as shown in **Figure 11-1**. One side of the button will be connected to ground (GND); the other is connected to the GPIO 14 pin (you can choose your favourite pin; just be sure to change the code). We used a breadboard for our stop-motion animation project, but you could wire the button directly to the pins (as you'll be doing for the selfie stick later).

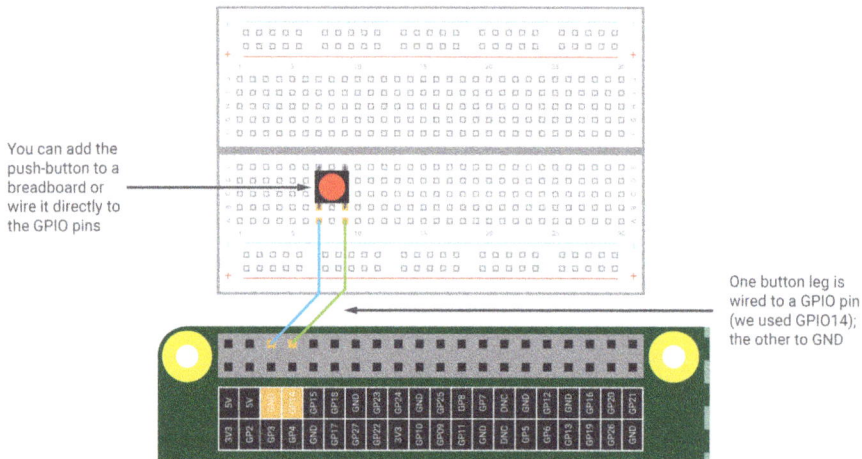

Figure 11-1 Connect the button

Install picamera

That's all the hardware done. Now it's time for the software. If you haven't done so already in Chapter 10, *Use Python with Picamera2*, you'll need to install the picamera2 library. In a Terminal window, enter:

```
$ sudo apt-get update
$ sudo apt install -y python3-picamera2
```

If for some reason you don't have GPIO Zero already installed (it has come pre-installed in Raspberry Pi OS for some time), do so with:

```
sudo apt-get install python-gpiozero python3-gpiozero
```

Stop-motion software

Because we're focusing on stop-motion for our first project, we're using the camera's preview mode so that we can set up our shot before we take it, to ensure everything is in the frame. Then, only when the button is pressed do we save an image file. Each image file will have a different name based on the date and time at which it is taken. This makes it easy to assemble all the images from the shoot for post-processing.

The wonderful GPIO Zero library is used to capture the button activity; we simply define a function that is run whenever the button is pressed. This function uses the Picamera2 Python library which allows us to control the camera through code, making all the normal command-line operations available.

Save the following code as **camera_stopmotion.py** and either run it through Thonny or from the command line (**python camera_stopmotion.py**). To quit the program, press **CTRL+C**. See *Welcome* on page v for details on downloading sample code.

```python
# Import the necessary modules
from datetime import datetime
from gpiozero import Button
from picamera2 import Picamera2, Preview
import time

b = Button(14)
cam = Picamera2()

# Configure the camera to capture in FHD with a VGA preview window.
config = cam.create_still_configuration(main={"size":(1920, 1080)},
                                        lores={"size":(640, 480)},
                                        display="lores")
cam.configure(config)

# Start the preview and the camera.
cam.start_preview(Preview.QTGL)
cam.start()

# Take a picture when the button is pressed.
def picture():
    time.sleep(.1) # Debounce (avoid counting one press as many)
    if b.is_pressed:
        # take the picture
        timestamp=datetime.now()
        cam.capture_file('pic'+str(timestamp)+'.jpg')
        print("Taken")
```

```
b.when_pressed = picture

try:
    print('Active')  # Let users know we're still running
    time.sleep(1)
# If we detect CTRL+C, then quit the program
except KeyboardInterrupt:
    cam.stop()
    cam.stop_preview()
```

Other variations

You should be able to use this code as a template to create a program for whatever photography project you have in mind. For example, you could alter the code so that the camera takes continuous photos while the button is held down. Or you could add extra buttons to make a variety of photography modes available.

With this sort of build, you can also start thinking about building a complete, portable, wirelessly connected Raspberry Pi camera. For this, you can use a case into which you can fit a portable mobile phone battery charger, along with a screen to attach to Raspberry Pi. With a bit of modification of the code, you can have it always show the preview of the camera on the screen. Want to record video? More modification of the code will allow for video capturing. The only issue you might have with both of these projects is the lack of a flash or built-in light source, so a well-lit subject would be essential.

Selfie stick

Next, we'll look at making a selfie stick. A lot of people roll their eyes and complain about vanity when it comes to the art of the selfie, but we all know it's nothing like that. New outfit? New glasses? Eyeliner wings perfectly symmetrical today? Why not chronicle it? It's a great confidence boost.

Our Raspberry Pi-powered selfie stick will use a similar hardware and software setup to the stop-motion animation project. As before, we're wiring up a push-button to GPIO 14 and GND pins on Raspberry Pi (see **Figure 11-2**), but this time we need to attach the jumpers to longer wires to put the button at the end of the 'stick' — we used a spatula, but anything long will do.

Your Raspberry Pi needs to be near to the camera (unless you've got an extra-long ribbon cable). Attach Raspberry Pi in a case to one end of the stick with

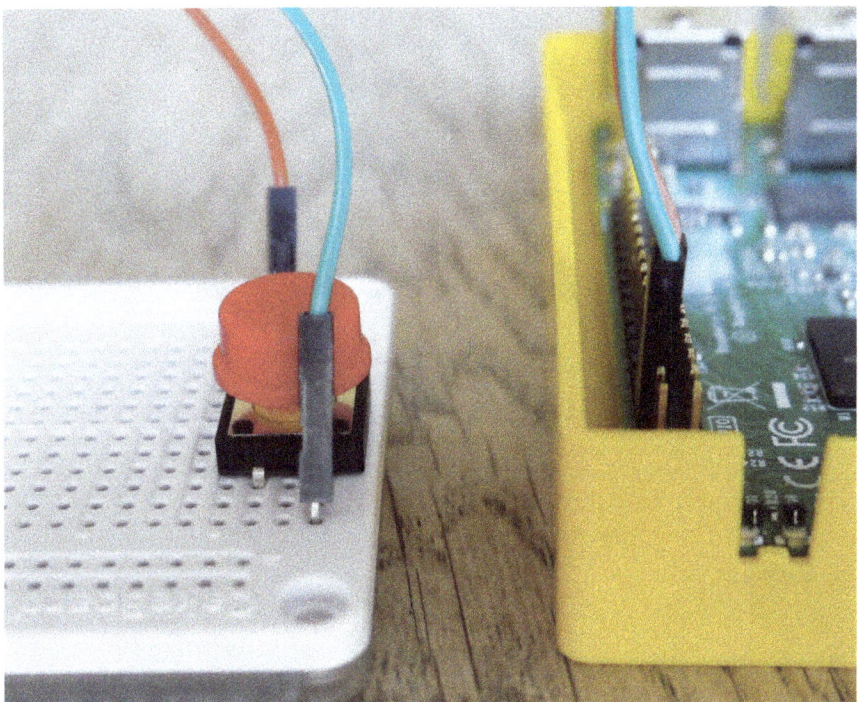

Figure 11-2 You can use a breadboard for a small button, or connect your jumper wires directly to the pins on a bigger one

whatever means you see fit (glue, adhesive putty, string, etc.) and then attach the button. The finished stick is shown in **Figure 11-3**.

Add the code

Since the principle is the same — pressing a button to take a photo — we can use the same code, **camera_stopmotion.py**, as for the stop-motion project. This time we don't need the camera preview, so you can comment out the line **cam.start_preview(Preview.QTGL)** if you like, by adding a **#** to the start of it.

Try running the code. Pressing the button will take a photo, but you'll need to practise your aim so you can get yourself in the frame (see **Figure 11-4**). As before, we add a timestamp to each picture, which helps to organise your pictures later and also results in a slight pause in the code, which at least means you won't take too many pictures with a slip of the button.

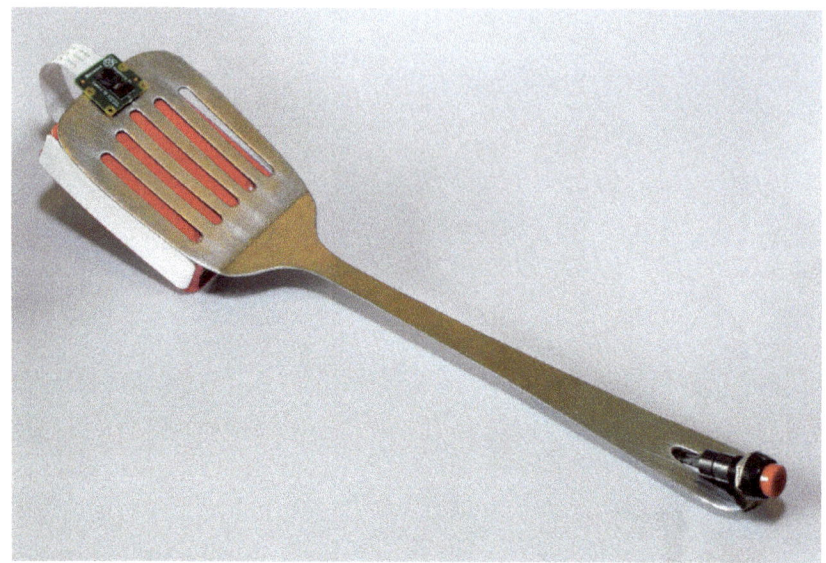

Figure 11-3 Our test selfie stick is very DIY, but you can use anything as long as you can attach a Raspberry Pi and have a long enough wire

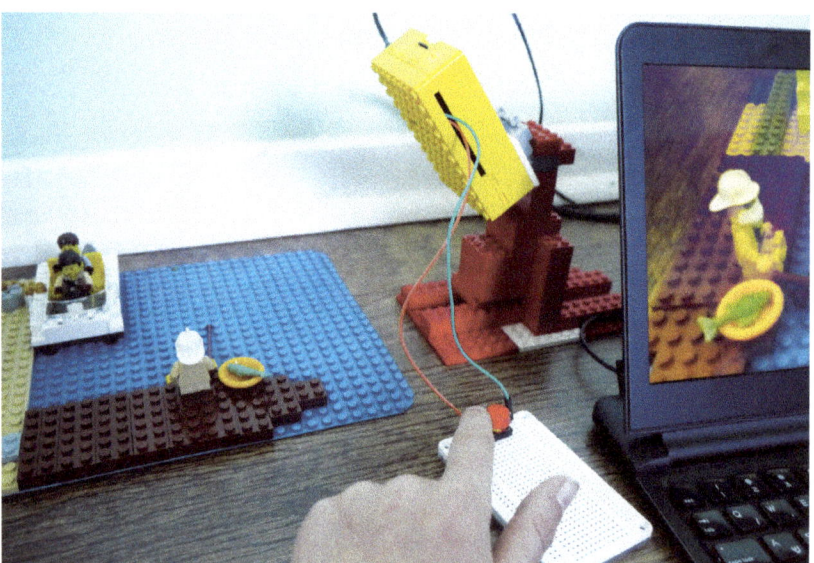

Figure 11-4 Create your stop-motion scene and use the button to trigger the camera to take pictures and save them to timestamped file

98 · Chapter 11 · **Stop-motion and selfies**

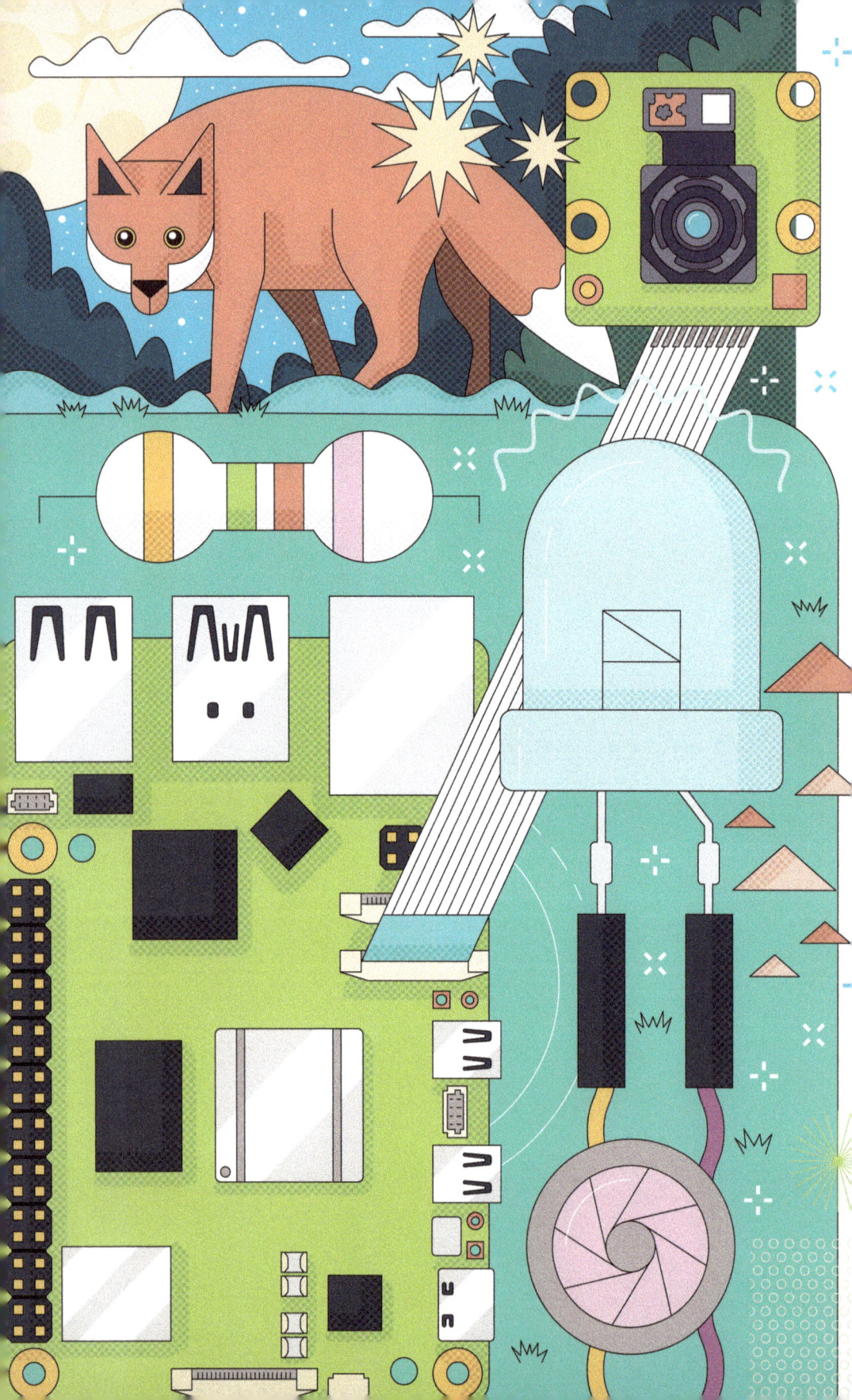

Chapter 12

Flash photography using an LED

Add an LED flash to shoot images in low light

The Raspberry Pi Camera Module and HQ Camera work well in good lighting, but what if there's less light available? Here we show you how to set up a simple LED flash, which you can trigger for each photo. We also look at how to shoot better images in low light without a flash.

What you'll need:

- Camera Module / HQ Camera
- Bright white LED
- Resistor (100Ω or greater)

Wire up an LED

Shut down your Raspberry Pi and disconnect the power. Next, connect a white LED — we used a 5 mm one — to your Raspberry Pi as shown in **Figure 12-1**. The LED's anode (long leg) is connected to GPIO 17, which we'll use to trigger the flash. To be sure of the LED not burning out from excess current, you should add a resistor of at least 100Ω between the LED's cathode (short leg) and GND.

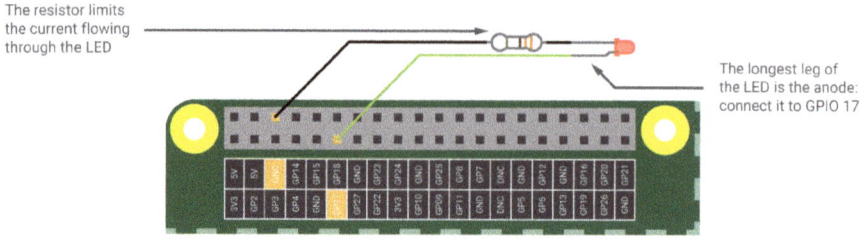

Figure 12-1 Connect an LED

If you want to use higher-powered or multiple LEDs, you'll have to think about powering them via a suitable driver circuit, with a transistor wired to the flash pin. You may also need a separate power supply. Note that, due to the rolling shutter in the standard Raspberry Pi Camera Module and HQ Camera, only an LED or equivalent flash is suitable: you can't use a xenon flash. Alternative flash/lighting methods include NeoPixel rings and the LISIPAROI light ring or similar 3rd-party accessories.

Flash the LED

To make your LED flash, you'll need to toggle the LED on and off manually in your code. It's best to leave the LED on briefly to let the camera's algorithms adapt to the light. Save the following code as **camera_led.py** and run it in the Terminal (**python camera_led.py**) or in Thonny (see *Welcome* on page v for details on downloading sample code):

```
import time
from picamera2 import Picamera2, Preview
from gpiozero import LED

cam = Picamera2()
flash_led = LED(17)

config = cam.create_still_configuration(main={"size":(1920, 1080)},
                                        lores={"size":(640, 480)},
                                        display="lores")
cam.configure(config)

cam.start_preview(Preview.QTGL)
cam.start()

flash_led.on()
```

```
time.sleep(1)  # Give the camera time to adapt to the lighting. Not
               # needed if you set gain/exposure/colour explicitly.

cam.capture_file("test.jpg")
flash_led.off()
cam.stop()
cam.stop_preview()
```

Depending on lighting conditions, you may find that the camera takes a while to settle down and take the picture. This happens because its automatic exposure and automatic white balance is adjusting to the level of illumination your LED provides (see **Figure 12-2**). If you set exposure and white balance levels manually, you'll take pictures much more quickly. If you add these lines after **time.sleep(1)**, it will show you the current analogue gain, exposure time, and colour gains:

```
md = cam.capture_metadata()
print(f"Analogue Gain: {md['AnalogueGain']}",
      f"ExposureTime: {md['ExposureTime']}",
      f"ColourGains: {md['ColourGains']}")
```

For example:

```
Analogue Gain: 2.0 ExposureTime: 11508
ColourGains: (1.405595302581787, 1.3223962783813477)
```

You can delete the lines you added, and add the following after the call to **cam.configure(config)**. Note that we're making only slight tweaks to the settings, as there is trial and error involved.

```
cam.set_controls({"AnalogueGain": 2.1,
                  "ExposureTime": 12000,
                  "ColourGains": (1.6, 1.1)
                 })
```

Low-light photography

In low-light scenarios where you don't want to use a flash, you can improve capture of images using a few tricks. By setting a high gain combined with a long exposure time, the camera is able to gather the maximum amount of light (see **Figure 12-3**). Note that since the **shutter_speed** attribute is constrained by the camera's frame rate, we need to set a very slow frame rate. The following code captures an image with a three-second exposure time: this is the maximum time for the Camera Module v1 — if you have a newer Camera

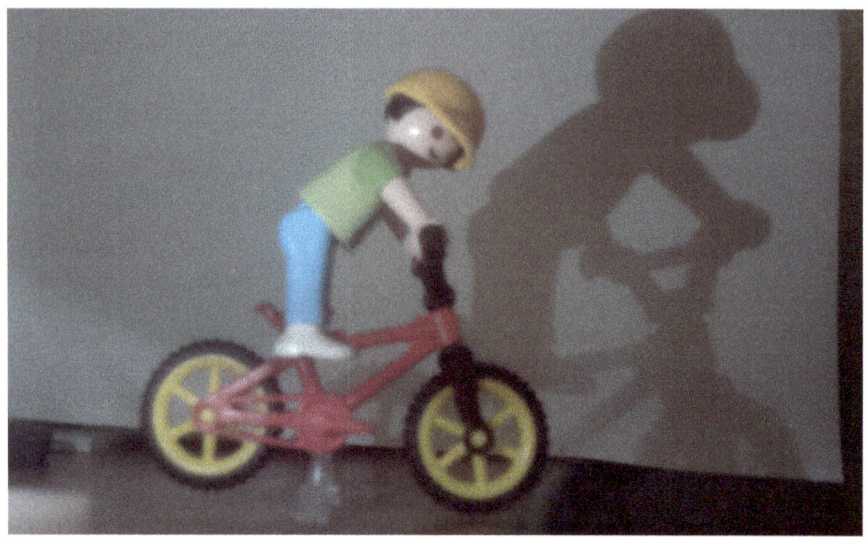

Figure 12-2 Even a single LED can provide illumination for close-up photography

Module, it can be extended to ten seconds, or much longer for an HQ Camera. Save the following program as **camera_led2.py** and run it:

```python
import time
from picamera2 import Picamera2, Preview
from gpiozero import LED

cam = Picamera2()
config = cam.create_still_configuration(main={"size":(1920, 1080)},
                                        lores={"size":(640, 480)},
                                        display="lores")
cam.configure(config)
cam.set_controls({"ExposureTime": 3000000,
                  "FrameRate": 1 / 6,
                  "AnalogueGain": 800 / 100
                  })

cam.start_preview(Preview.QTGL)
cam.start()

# Give the camera a good long time to set gains and
# measure AWB (you may wish to use fixed AWB instead)
time.sleep(30)
```

```
# Finally, capture an image with a 6s exposure. Due
# to mode switching on the still port, this will take
# longer than six seconds
cam.capture_file("dark.jpg")
cam.stop()
cam.stop_preview()
```

The frame rate is set to a sixth of a second, while we set the ISO to 800 (the ISO is the gain multiplied by 100) for greater exposure. A pause of 30 seconds gives the camera enough time to set gains and measure AWB (auto white balance).

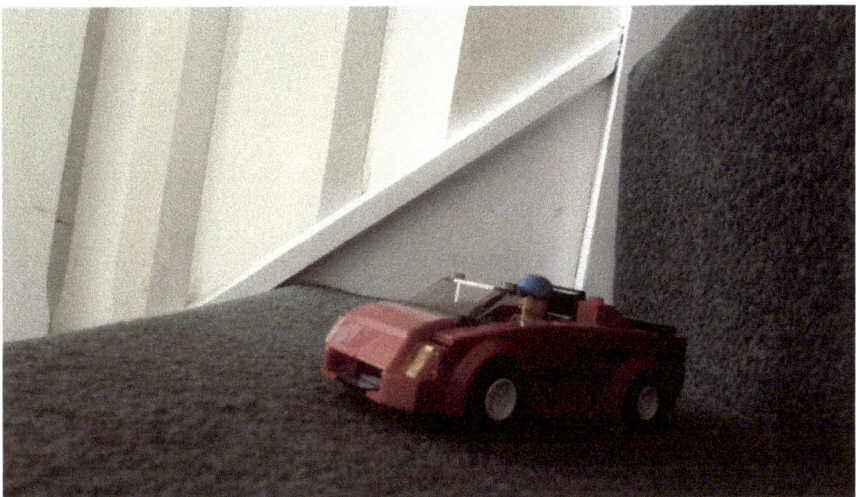

Figure 12-3 Using a long exposure, you can shoot stills in very dark settings

Try running the script in a very dark setting: it may take some time to run, including the 30-second pause and about 20 seconds for the capture itself.

The particular camera settings in this script are only useful for very low light conditions: in a well-lit environment, the image produced will be heavily overexposed, so you may need to increase the frame rate and lower the shutter speed accordingly.

If the image has a green cast, you'll need to alter the white balance manually. You can set the red/blue gains manually; e.g. `cam.set_controls({"Colour-Gains": (1.6, 1.1)})`.

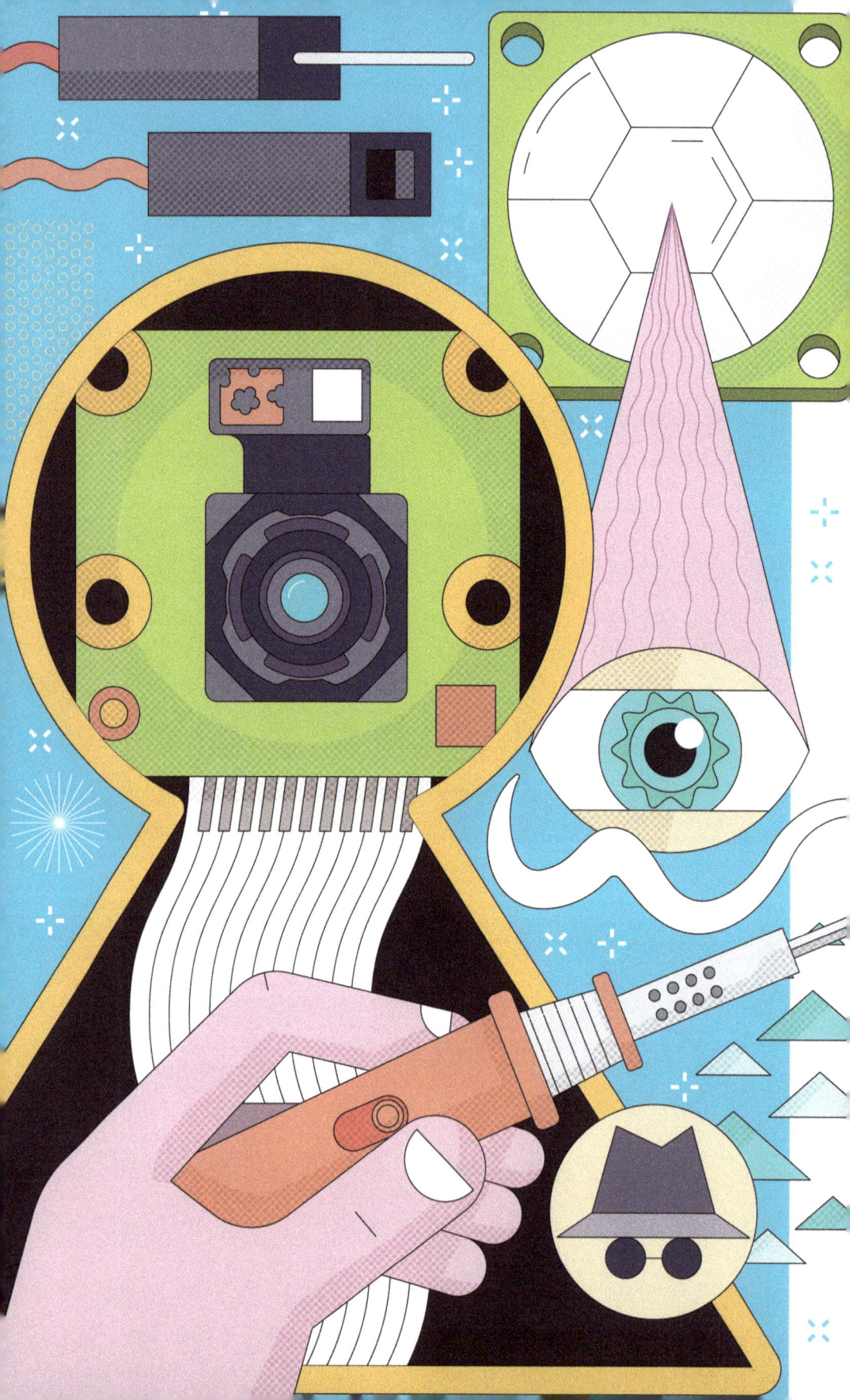

Chapter 13

Make a spy camera

Set up a motion-activated spy camera in your room

We've all been there. You've gone out for the day and you know you closed your bedroom door, but you come back and it's slightly ajar. Who's been in there? Were they friend or foe? In this chapter we'll use the Camera Module or HQ Camera as a spy camera that takes a picture when anyone's presence is detected by a passive infrared (PIR) sensor. Here we're using a Raspberry Pi Zero — which is easier to hide away due to its size — with a special camera cable for it, but you can use any Raspberry Pi model. Unless you want to power it from the mains, you'll also need a portable power supply such as a mobile phone battery pack.

You'll need

- Camera Module / HQ Camera
- PIR sensor (see **magpi.cc/pir**)
- Raspberry Pi 5/Zero camera cable (optional: **magpi.cc/zerocamcable**)
- Portable power supply (optional)
- Jumper wires

Getting started

First, make sure your Camera Module or HQ Camera is connected to your Raspberry Pi (see "Connecting and testing your camera" on page 10). If you haven't done so already in Chapter 10, *Use Python with Picamera2*, you'll need to install the Picamera2 library. In a Terminal window, enter:

```
sudo apt update
sudo apt install -y python3-picamera2
```

Wire up the circuit

Before you wire the circuit, shut down your Raspberry Pi and unplug it from power. The circuit for this is fairly simple, especially as the PIR does not need a resistor as part of its setup. The PIR comes with three connection pins: VCC, GND, and OUT (sometimes labelled SIG for signal). If you can't find their labels on the bottom of the sensor, lift off the plastic golf-ball-like diffuser and you should see them on the top of the board. If you're using a model that requires 5V power, VCC needs to be connected to a 5V power pin. Some PIR sensors use 3.3V power; if yours does, you should power it from the 3V3 pin instead.

Next, GND needs to go to a ground pin, and then there's the OUT wire which will be our input. We're connecting it to GPIO 14. Regardless of the input voltage, you should make sure that your PIR's signal *output* is at 3.3V, as Raspberry Pi's GPIO pins do not tolerate more than that. Check the website or datasheet for your PIR to confirm.

If your Raspberry Pi Zero has GPIO pins attached, you can use female-to-female jumper wires to make the connections, as shown in **Figure 13-1**. Otherwise, you can loop the wire around the GPIO holes and use a bit of putty to keep them in place, or a dab of glue from a glue gun on a low setting. Soldering is an option if you want to create a permanent spy camera device.

Write the code

Now that you've got it all wired up, it's time to start coding your spy camera. In the Thonny code editor, create a new file with the following code, save it as **camera_spycam.py**, and run it.

You can also create this file in any editor and run it from the command line (`python camera_spycam.py`) or download it from the book's GitHub repository (see *Welcome* on page v for details on downloading sample code).

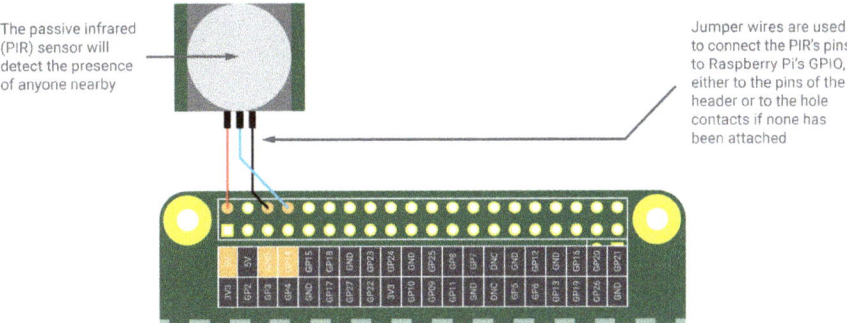

Figure 13-1 Connect a PIR sensor

```
from gpiozero import MotionSensor
from picamera2 import Picamera2
from datetime import datetime
import time

sensor = MotionSensor(14)
cam = Picamera2()
cam.start()

time_format = "%H.%M.%S_%Y-%m-%d.jpg"
while True:
    sensor.wait_for_motion()
    filename = datetime.now().strftime(time_format)
    cam.capture_file(filename)
    print(f"Captured {filename}")
    time.sleep(5)
```

This script uses two libraries: GPIO Zero and the standard Picamera2 library. You use GPIO Zero to get a reading from the PIR motion sensor. Each time the sensor detects motion, the code uses the Picamera library to take a photo.

At the top, we import **MotionSensor** from GPIO Zero and **Picamera2** from the **picamera2** library. Since we'll be giving each photo a timestamp, we also import **datetime**, along with the **time** library.

In a never-ending **while True:** loop, we use GPIO Zero's **wait_for_motion** function to pause the code until the PIR detects any motion. When it does, we set the photo file name to the current time and date, then take the picture. To enable the PIR to settle, we sleep for five seconds before returning to the top of the loop to wait for motion again.

Final preparations

You can run the code first to give it a test. You might want to change the sensitivity and/or trigger time, which you can do on most PIR boards by adjusting the little orange potentiometer screws on the side of the board: Sx adjusts sensitivity, while Tx alters the trigger time.

Once that's done, you'll want to get the program to start automatically whenever you boot up the Raspberry Pi. To do so, open up a Terminal window and edit your *cron table* with `crontab -e`. You may be asked to select an editor the first time you run this command. When the editor appears, go to the bottom of the file, and add this line:

`@reboot /usr/bin/python camera_spycam.py`

This assumes you saved the **camera_spycam.py** file in your home directory. If you put it in a subdirectory, such as **~/spycam**, you would need to change directory for the duration of the command, in which case you'd add something like this instead:

`@reboot (cd spycam; /usr/bin/python camera_spycam.py)`

This will ensure that the script runs under your user credentials each time the system boots.

Boot your Pi to the CLI

In addition, to get Raspberry Pi to boot up slightly faster and to use a little less power so your battery lasts longer, it's best to get it to boot directly to the command line rather than booting to the desktop. The easiest way to change this is to click the Raspberry menu, choose **Preferences** and select **Raspberry Pi Configuration**; in the **System** tab, change **Boot** to the **To CLI** option. Alternatively, open a Terminal window and enter `sudo raspi-config` to open the Configuration Tool; select **System Options**, then **Boot / Auto Login**, and select **Console Autologin Text Console**, then select **Finish** and reboot. This boots to the text console and logs you in automatically, and the spycam script runs in the background.

To stop the script while it's running, you can run the following command. Unlike `pidof`, which only searches the name of the executable, `pgrep -f` searches a process' command-line arguments, including the script name:

`kill $(pgrep -f camera_spycam.py)`

Deploy your camera

Now you need to find a good place to hide your camera. The default cable for the camera is limited by length, while the PIR will work with fairly long jumper wires, so keep that in mind when building your system. Alternatively, you could get a camera extender (**magpi.cc/camextender**) to link your cable to a standard-width one. Longer standard-width cables — of up to 2 m — are also available if you are not using a Raspberry Pi Zero.

Hiding your Raspberry Pi and battery behind a plush toy or photo frame can work well (you could even put a dummy photo up and cut a hole in it for the camera to look through). The PIR has quite a wide range, so put it up high where people are unlikely to look.

Check for intruders

All you need to do now is plug in the power supply and your Raspberry Pi will turn on and automatically run the script. Do some tests to make sure the camera is facing the right way. Leave it running during the day and then when you get back, plug it into a monitor, stop the script, and run **startx** to get the GUI up, or use **sftp** from a remote computer to transfer files over. From here you can see the pictures it has taken (see **Figure 13-2**) — crucial evidence to catch your dog or sibling red-handed.

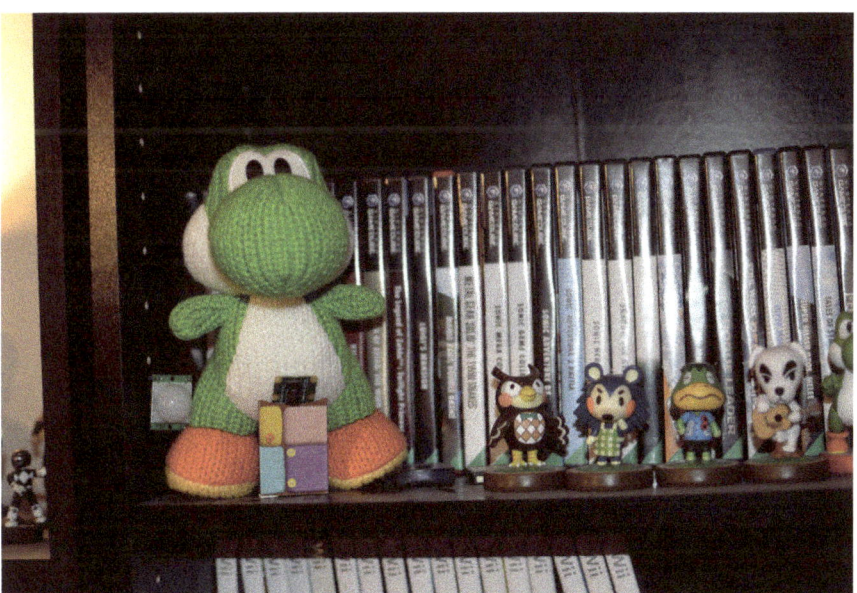

Figure 13-2 Camouflaged against Yoshi, the camera will take candid snaps of anyone who comes close to your game collection

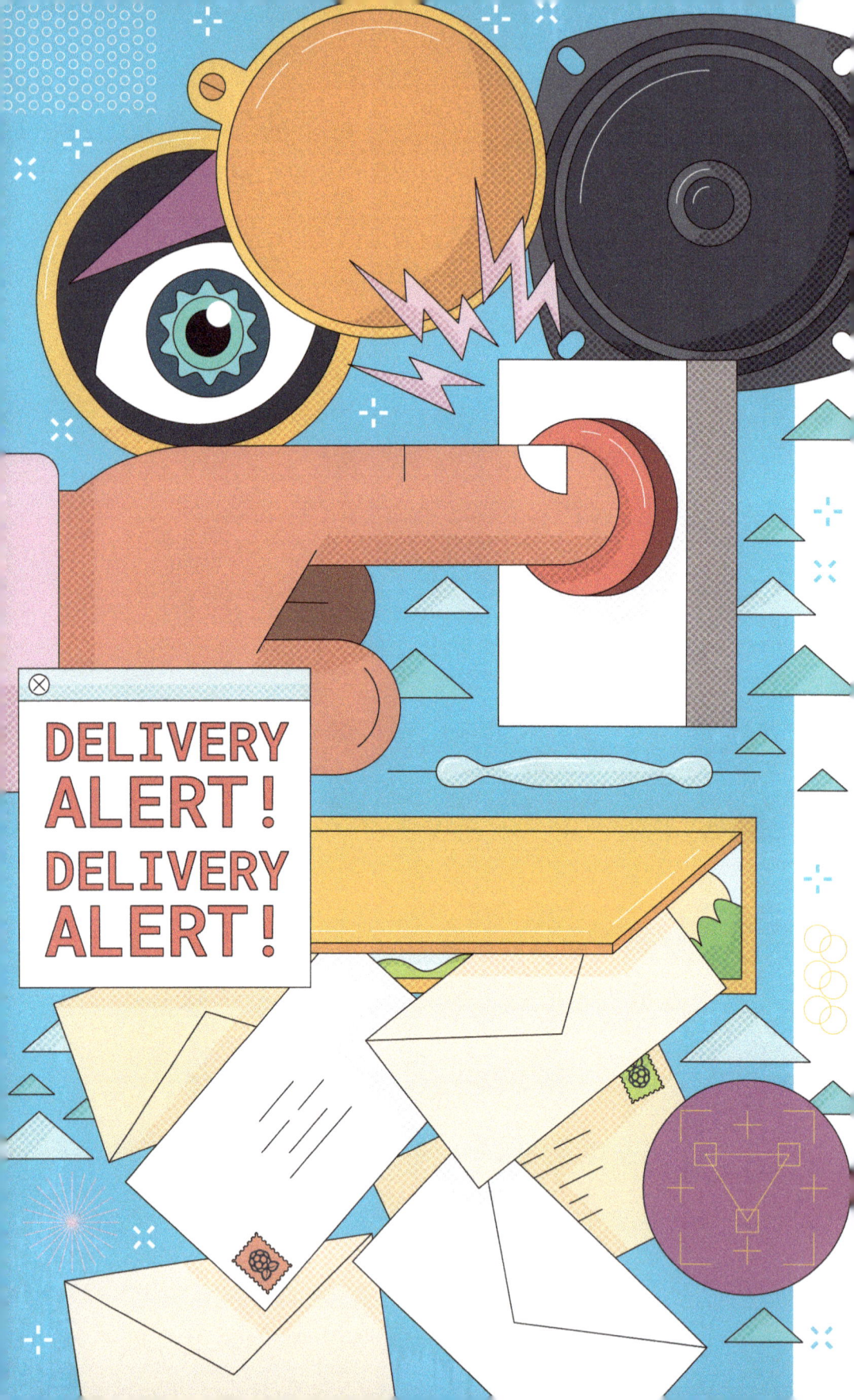

Chapter 14

Smart door

Add a Raspberry Pi to your door with magical results

Is your door a bore? Open and close, open and close. Snoozefest. Surely it can do more than that? How about a smart door that knows when someone approaches, when the post arrives, and can even offer remote viewing of the peephole? You could even add intelligent lighting, a controllable door lock, and facial recognition, all powered with your Raspberry Pi. So, let's ignore super-expensive door systems and build our own. You can do as much, or as little, as you like of this project and there's plenty of room for new and inventive uses.

You'll need

- A (preferably small) HDMI monitor with built-in or external speakers
- Camera Module / HQ Camera
- PIR sensor (**magpi.cc/pir**)
- 2 × Security door contact reed switch (**magpi.cc/doorswitch**)
- Wired doorbell (**magpi.cc/wiredbell**)

> **Night is dark**
>
> If you want the camera to work well at night, you may want to consider a Pi NoIR Camera Module supported with some infrared lighting.

Prepare your Raspberry Pi

Start by connecting your Raspberry Pi to the monitor and, if needed connecting an external speaker (for the doorbell sound). In the Raspberry Pi desktop, right-click the volume icon in the upper left and make sure HDMI is selected.

If you haven't done so already in Chapter 10, *Use Python with Picamera2*, you'll need to install the Picamera2 library. In a Terminal window, enter:

```
sudo apt update
sudo apt install -y python3-picamera2
```

Attach the camera

This part will be easier if your camera is *not* connected to your Raspberry Pi right now. Power off your Raspberry Pi and unplug it from power.

We're going to keep an eye on the outside world by replacing the door's peephole with the Raspberry Pi camera. A peephole is typically a two-piece barrel that screws together and can be easily unscrewed from the inside. Remove the barrel and cover the hole with the camera. Affix the camera with whatever is handy; gaffer tape is a great temporary or permanent solution.

Mount or place the monitor and Raspberry Pi somewhere near the door, but make sure the Raspberry Pi is close enough to the camera for camera's ribbon cable to reach. Next, connect your Camera Module or HQ Camera to your Raspberry Pi (see "Connecting and testing your camera" on page 10).

Figure 14-1 shows our prototype. We used the Raspberry Pi Touch Display (**magpi.cc/touch**) a PAM8302 amplifier (**magpi.cc/pam8302**), and powered speaker (**magpi.cc/3inspeaker**). If you're using an HDMI monitor, you'll find it easier to use its built-in speaker or plug in an external speaker.

Footsteps approaching!

The first smart thing our door is going to do is detect someone approaching it. A PIR sensor is perfect for the job. These cool little geodesic domes are triggered by heat and are the same gizmos that you find in motion-sensing lights and security systems. Connect to Raspberry Pi as shown in **Figure 14-2**, but make sure that your PIR uses 3.3V logic levels so as not to overload the GPIOs (if your PIR requires a 3.3V power *source*, connect its positive lead to the 3V3 pin instead of 5V). See "Wire up the circuit" on page 108 for more details. You can usually control the sensitivity and duration of a 'detection' with two potentiometers on the PIR board. Mount the PIR outside in a suitable location to monitor your door.

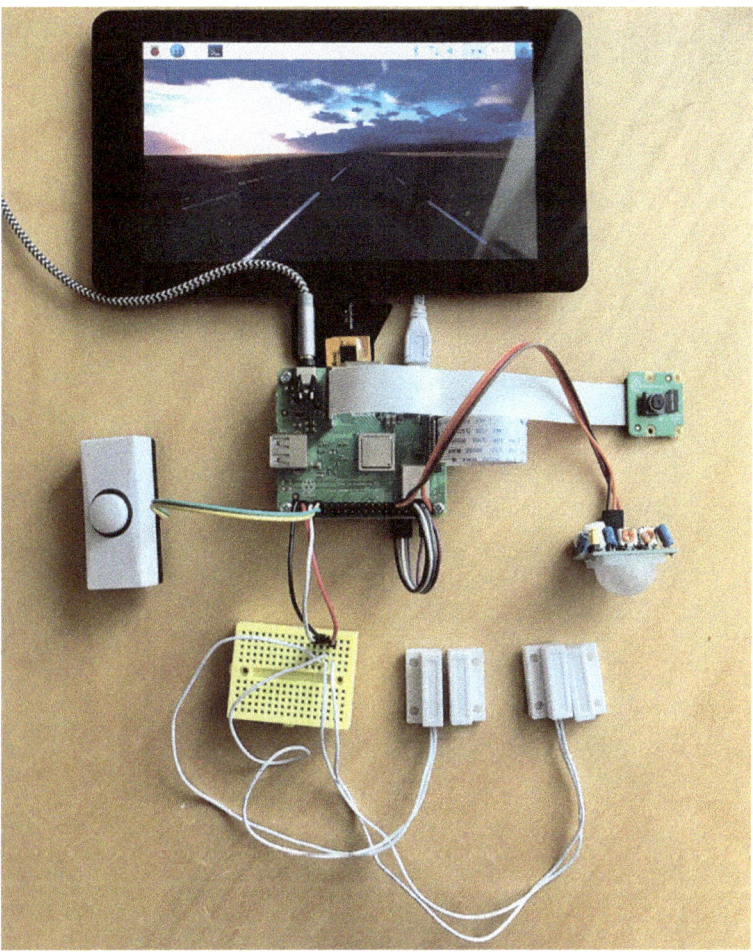

Figure 14-1   You may want to prototype this project and test it before taking a drill to your door!

Monitor the door and letterbox

We have two magnetic reed switches, the type you find on windows and doors for security systems. They are made up of two parts: the wired part is a reed switch and the unwired a magnet. When the magnet meets the switch, it closes. If we attach the magnet to the door and the switch to the frame, when the door opens, so does the switch. There's no polarity to worry about, so connect one wire to GPIO 26 and the other to the adjacent GND. Repeat for the letterbox using GPIO 19. You may need a breadboard.

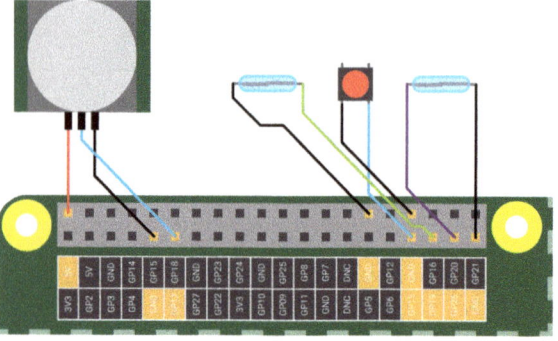

Figure 14-2 The GPIO wiring that's needed for the various inputs and outputs

Ding dong!

If we replace the doorbell with our own button, we can take a photo with the Camera Module or HQ Camera when someone presses it and send a notification. Way better. Mount a standard wired doorbell, which after all is just a momentary contact button, to the outside door frame and wire it back to Raspberry Pi using GPIO 13 and an available GND pin. If you're prototyping on a breadboard, a tactile switch will do fine.

Figure 14-3 shows the installed smart door system in all its glory.

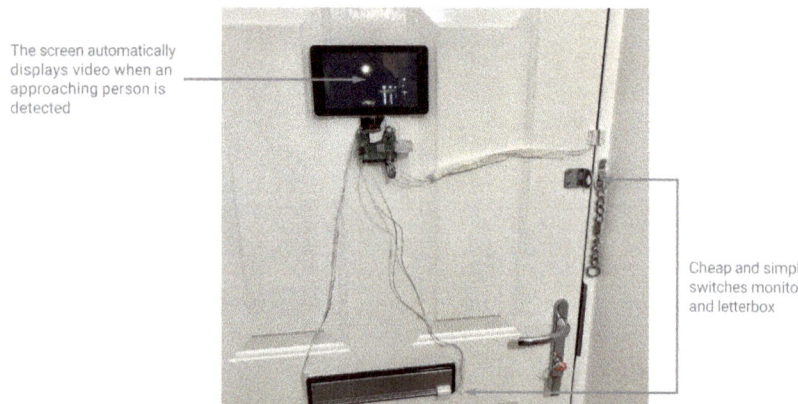

Figure 14-3 Our smart door contraption fixed in position

Code

Double-check all your connections and then power up your Raspberry Pi. You'll need to download a doorbell sound into the **smartdoor** subdirectory:

```
mkdir ~/smartdoor
curl -o ~/smartdoor/doorbell.mp3 -L https://magpi.cc/doorbellmp3
```

Create a file in Thonny with the code from "smartdoor_test.py" on page 118 and save it as **smartdoor_test.py**. You can also create that file in any editor and run it from the command line or download it from the book's GitHub repository (see *Welcome* on page v).

Watch the console output. If everything is working, you should be able to trigger the PIR, the reed switches, and the doorbell. The camera will capture ten seconds of video when motion is detected, and a photo when the doorbell is pressed. These are both saved to the desktop.

But wait, there's more!

There are a lot of ways you can build on this sample project. Here are a few ideas to get you started on customising your own smart door:

Get alerts!
> How would you like to have your smart door notify you wherever you are? You can use an app called Pushover, which makes it easy to receive push notifications on your phone. Follow the Pushover documentation (**pushover.net/api**) to register and get your API credentials. Next, check out their Python examples (**magpi.cc/pushover-python**) and integrate that code with your own program.

Facial recognition
> Once a futuristic technology, decent facial recognition is now well within the grasp of Raspberry Pi. Using the doorbell photo taken by Raspberry Pi, you can recognise a face using reference photos. A familiar face could even trigger the lock, or you could play a welcome announcement. There are many ways to add facial recognition to your Python programs, such as with the `face_recognition` Python library (check out **magpi.cc/HSfacialrec** for an example of its use).

Door lock
> If you're interested in being able to control your door's lock, you may see that some solutions are very pricey. One that is perfect for experimentation is the *magnetic hold lock*, which uses an electromagnet to hold the

door closed. The one we've used (**magpi.cc/magneticaccess**) can withstand 180 kg of force, although stronger ones are available.

The magnet mounts on the door and the electromagnet on the frame. The provided PSU contains a relay that can be powered by Raspberry Pi by connecting it to a spare GPIO line and ground. Please note this is no replacement for a proper door lock system. Magnetic door locks vary in size and shape, so measure twice and order once!

smartdoor_test.py

```python
from picamera2 import Picamera2, Preview
from picamera2.encoders import H264Encoder
from gpiozero import Button, MotionSensor
from pygame import mixer
import time
import os
import pathlib

# Set up the devices
cam = Picamera2()
motion = MotionSensor(17)
doorSensor = Button(26)
letterbox = Button(19)
doorbell = Button(13)
mixer.init()

# Set up filenames
home = pathlib.Path.home()
vidfile = os.path.join(home, 'Desktop', 'motion.h264')
bellfile = os.path.join(home, 'smartdoor', 'doorbell.mp3')
picfile = os.path.join(home, 'Desktop', 'doorbell.jpg')
mixer.music.load(bellfile)

recording = False
photographing = False
def motionDetected():
    global recording, photographing
    while photographing:
        time.sleep(1) # wait until the photo is done
    print("Motion detected, video recording")
    recording = True
    cam.start_and_record_video(vidfile, show_preview=True)
    time.sleep(10)
```

```python
def motionStopped():
    global recording
    # Make sure we're really recording, because the sensor may
    # have already been active when you started the program.
    if recording:
        print("Stopping video recording")
        cam.stop_recording()
        cam.stop_preview()
        recording = False

def doorOpen():
    print("Door open")

def doorClosed():
    print("Door closed")

def letterboxOpen():
    print("You've got mail!")

def doorbellPressed():
    global recording, photographing
    while recording: # Wait until the video is done
        time.sleep(1)
    mixer.music.play()
    photographing = True
    cam.start_and_capture_file(picfile)
    photographing = False
    print("Someone's at the door!")

# Attach our functions to GPIO Zero events
motion.when_motion = motionDetected
motion.when_no_motion = motionStopped
doorSensor.when_pressed = doorClosed
doorSensor.when_released = doorOpen
letterbox.when_released = letterboxOpen
doorbell.when_released = doorbellPressed

print("Smart door is smart")
# Loop forever allowing events to do their thing
try:
    while True:
        pass
except KeyboardInterrupt:
    print("Smart door no longer smart")
```

This Python program uses **picamera2** to manage the camera, GPIO Zero to manage sensors and buttons, and **pygame** (a Python game library) to play the audio file. After importing those (and other) libraries, the program sets up the input devices and creates filenames for the doorbell sound and for the video and picture files that it will capture to.

The **motionDetected** function is called when the PIR sensor detects a presence, and it uses the **recording** and **photographing** global flags to make sure that other functions don't try to do something with the camera at the same time. This function uses the **start_and_record_video** function from Picamera2's high-level API, which doesn't require as much setup as examples from previous chapters.

When the PIR goes low (is no longer detecting a presence), the program triggers the **motionStopped** function, which stops the recording. The **doorOpen**, **doorClosed**, and **letterBoxOpen** functions each print a message for their respective events.

The **doorbellPressed** function uses the **recording** and **photographing** global variables to make sure it doesn't clash with other functions. It plays the doorbell sound, takes a photo (also using a high-level API function, **start_and_capture_file**), and prints a message. At the bottom there are a few lines of code that connect those functions with the corresponding GPIO Zero events, followed by a loop that keeps running until you stop the program with **CTRL+C** (or click the **Stop** button in Thonny).

Here we've given you the basics to get going, but more complex events are possible. You could alert different people based on facial recognition or play custom doorbell tones. And, if you had problems with deliveries, video evidence can build up automatically. On a serious note, remember a lot of this is 'just for fun' and designed to inspire, so unless you're prepared to put in the work hardening the code and including failsafes, don't rely on this, or possibly make it as a fun kids' door project (but maybe without the lock!).

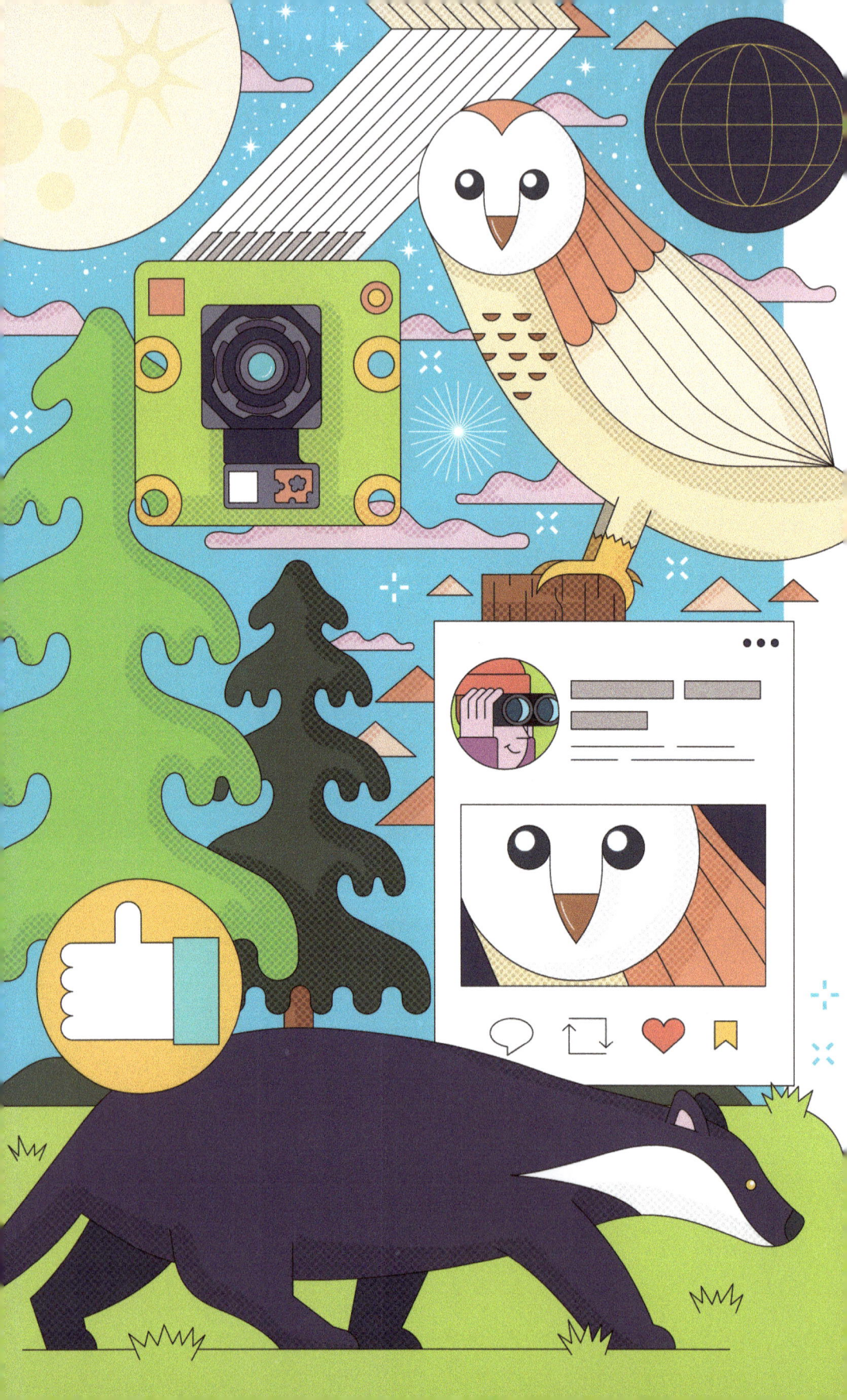

Chapter 15

Build a wildlife camera trap

Uncover the goings-on in your garden

Ever wondered what lurks at the bottom of your garden at night, or which furry friends are visiting the school playground once all the children have gone home? Using a Raspberry Pi and Camera Module (or HQ Camera), along with an object-recognition toolkit, is a cheap but effective way to capture some excellent close-ups of foxes, birds, mice, squirrels, and badgers.

You'll need

- Camera Module / HQ Camera
- Raspberry Pi NoIR Camera Module (optional)
- ZeroCam NightVision (optional)
- Waterproof container (like a jam jar)
- Blu Tack, Sugru, elastic bands, carabiners, or zip ties

Prepare your Raspberry Pi

First, make sure your camera is connected to your Raspberry Pi (see "Connecting and testing your camera" on page 10). The Camera Module or HQ Camera will work in some environments, but if you choose the NoIR Camera Module (**magpi.cc/ircamera**), you'll get better results in the dark. PiHut's ZeroCam NightVision (**magpi.cc/zerocamnight**) combines a NoIR-style camera with two powerful infrared emitters that will really let you see in the dark!

If you haven't done so already in Chapter 10, *Use Python with Picamera2*, you'll need to install the Picamera2 library. In a Terminal window, enter:

```
sudo apt update
sudo apt install -y python3-picamera2
```

Object detection with YOLO

There are many different object-detection libraries available, but we chose the Ultralytics distribution of YOLO (*You Only Look Once*) because of its excellent documentation and ease of use on Raspberry Pi.

Before you can install a third-party Python library such as YOLO, you'll need to set up a Python *virtual environment*. This lets you install optional libraries without affecting your main Python environment.

The simplest thing to do is set up an environment under your user account. Use the following command to create a virtual environment in the **env** folder in your home directory:

```
python -m venv --system-site-packages ~/env
```

Next, you can run the following command from any directory to start using the virtual environment (you'll need to run this for each new Terminal window, SSH session, or console login):

```
source ~/env/bin/activate
```

You should then see a prompt like the following:

```
(env) username@hostname:~ $
```

To leave the virtual environment, run the following command from any directory:

```
deactivate
```

You can find instructions for other configurations, such as per-project environments, at **rptl.io/venv**. If you don't feel like running the command `source ~/env/bin/activate` every time you want to use the environment, you could add that line to your **~/.profile**.

Now you're ready to install the Ultralytics YOLO distribution. Make sure you see the `(env)` prompt (if not, run the `source` command shown earlier to load the virtual environment). Run the following command:

```
pip install -U pip
pip install ultralytics[export]
```

The first command updates **pip** (the package installer for Python) to the latest version and the second installs Ultralytics. It may take some time for this installation to complete. Reboot your Raspberry Pi when it's done.

You can test your Ultralytics installation with this command (don't forget to run **source ~/env/bin/activate** after you open a new Terminal window):

```
yolo predict model=yolo11n.pt source=https://magpi.cc/objdetect.jpg
```

The first time you run this, it will download the **yolo11n.pt** model into your current working directory, so you need to be online for that first time. When it's done, it should create a file named **objdetect.jpg** in the **runs/detect/predict** subdirectory underneath your current working directory. Open that file and you'll see that it's been labelled, as shown in **Figure 15-1**. Each time you run a prediction, it will add a number to the predict directory, as in **runs/detect/predict1**, **runs/detect/predict2**, etc.

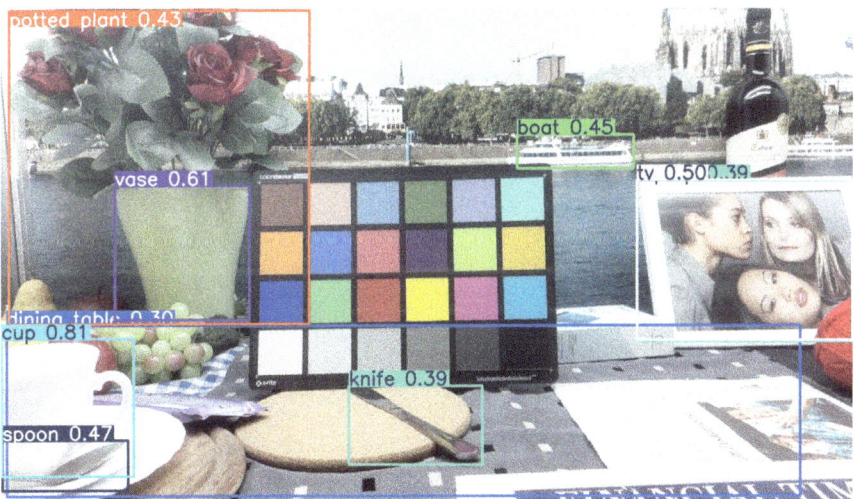

Figure 15-1 Framing and labelling detected objects

The Code

With the Ultralytics Python libraries, you can take pictures using the Picamera2 library and look for objects in them. In the Thonny code editor, create a new file with the following code, and save it as **camera_wildlife.py**. You can also create this file in any editor or download it from the book's GitHub repository (see *Welcome* on page v for details on downloading sample code).

```python
from datetime import datetime
from picamera2 import Picamera2
from ultralytics import YOLO
import time
import os
import cv2

# Initialize and configure the camera
cam = Picamera2()
config = cam.create_still_configuration(main={"size":(1280, 720),
                                              "format": "RGB888"})
cam.align_configuration(config)
cam.configure(config)
cam.start()

# Download (if necessary) and load the YOLO11 model.
model = YOLO("yolo11n.pt")
names = model.names

threshold = .40 # Minimum confidence required to consider a match.
folder = "wildlife"
os.makedirs(folder, exist_ok = True) # A folder to store images.

def capture_objects(previous_classes):
    # Capture a frame from the camera.
    img = cam.capture_array()
    ts = str(datetime.now()) # get a timestamp

    # Run the inference on that image.
    results = model(img)

    # Add boxes and labels to the image.
    annotated = results[0].plot()

    # Get all the boxes (one for each object identified), the
    # class names, and confidence levels.
    boxes = results[0].boxes.xyxy.cpu().tolist()
```

```python
        clss = results[0].boxes.cls.cpu().tolist()
        confs = results[0].boxes.conf.cpu().tolist()

        # Iterate over each object.
        if boxes is not None:
            if set(clss) == previous_classes:
                print("Scene is unchanged, not saving images.")
                return set(clss)

            for box, cls, conf in zip(boxes, clss, confs):
                if conf < threshold: # Is confidence under threshold?
                    continue

                # Crop the image to the current object.
                crop = img[int(box[1]) : int(box[3]),
                           int(box[0]) : int(box[2])]
                clssname = names[int(cls)] # get the object class name

                # Save each object in its class folder.
                clss_folder = os.path.join(folder, clssname)
                os.makedirs(clss_folder, exist_ok = True)
                filename = os.path.join(clss_folder, ts) + ".jpg"
                cv2.imwrite(filename, crop)

            # Save the original and the annotated version.
            image_basename = os.path.join(folder, ts)
            cv2.imwrite(image_basename + ".jpg", img)
            cv2.imwrite(image_basename + "-annotated.jpg", annotated)

        return set(clss)

# Start the main loop
previous_classes = set()
try:
    while True:
        previous_classes = capture_objects(previous_classes)
        time.sleep(10)
except KeyboardInterrupt: # If you press CTRL+C, quit the program.
    print("Received CTRL+C, shutting down.")
    cam.stop()
```

Now it's time to run the script. You'll need to run this script using the virtual environment you created earlier. If you're running it from the command line, be sure to run **source ~/env/bin/activate** if you haven't already. Next, run it from the command line (**python camera_wildlife.py**).

To run it in Thonny, you'll need to tell Thonny to use your virtual environment:

1. Click on **Local Python 3 /usr/bin/python3** in the lower-right corner of the Thonny window, then click **Configure Interpreter**.
2. In the **Thonny Options** dialogue that appears, click the **...** button to the right of the Python executable.
3. A directory picker dialogue appears. Navigate to the **env** subdirectory under your home directory, go into the bin subdirectory, and double-click on **python3**.
4. Click **OK** to close the **Thonny Options** dialog, and you'll be able to run **camera_wildlife.py** from Thonny.

The program starts out simple enough by importing some libraries. Next, it configures and starts the camera. After that, it loads the YOLO model, downloading it if necessary (this means you need to be online the first time you run the program). Next, it initialises a variable (`names`), an array that contains all the class names (flowerpot, car, boat, etc.) in the model. We'll use that later.

The program then sets a variable named `threshold`, which is the minimum confidence level needed for the program to save an image of an object. The program then creates a subdirectory, **wildlife**, to store all the images.

The `capture_objects` function definition follows. This takes one argument, `previous_classes`, which is a set of the classes from the last time the function was called. The function takes a picture, runs an inference on it to identify objects, then annotates the image with labels and boxes to surround each object. The label includes the name of the class of object it found along with the confidence level.

Next, the function goes through all the individual objects that it identified. If the set of classes found last time (`previous_classes`) is identical to the current set, it returns and doesn't save anything. If you want to see multiple pictures of the same critter, you might want to change this logic!

If it finds an object that satisfies the confidence level threshold, it then saves the object to a subdirectory for that class of object under **wildlife**. After that's done, the function saves the original captured image along with the annotated one in the **wildlife** subdirectory.

The program's main loop runs forever, calling `capture_objects` until you press **CTRL+C**. After the program has run for a while and encountered some visitors, you'll end up with some captured images, along with individual photos stored in a subdirectory corresponding to the class of object, in a time-stamped image. You can use SSH to access these files remotely or run a web server (see "Launch a web server" on page 78) to make them accessible from any web browser.

Deploying the camera

Next, you need to install your Raspberry Pi and camera somewhere outside and connect it to your battery bank. You'll want some kind of waterproof container to put it all in; choose something that the Camera Module can see through.

Figure 15-2 shows the camera equipment we set up when we built this project. We used the ZeroCam NightVision from PiHut as our camera, an external power bank, and put it all in some watertight containers. You can see some of our results in **Figure 15-3** and **Figure 15-4**. Here's hoping you find interesting, fun, and friendly critters in the images you capture!

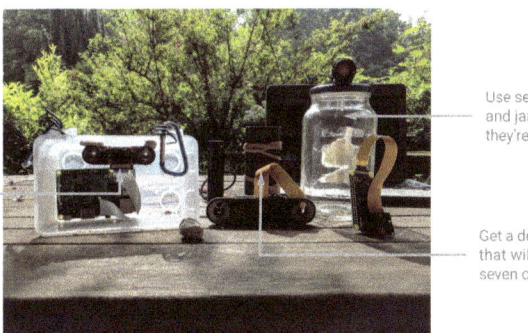

Figure 15-2 Wildlife camera capture equipment

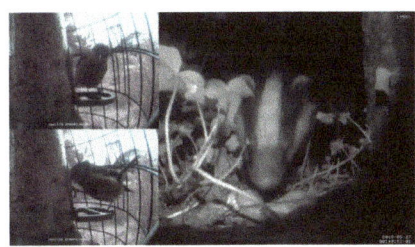

Figure 15-3
Unleash your inner Springwatch

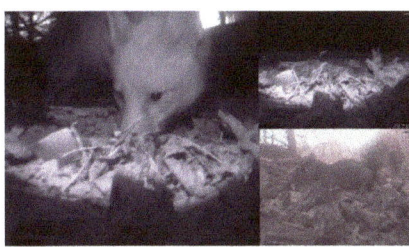

Figure 15-4
Get great photos with night-vision cameras

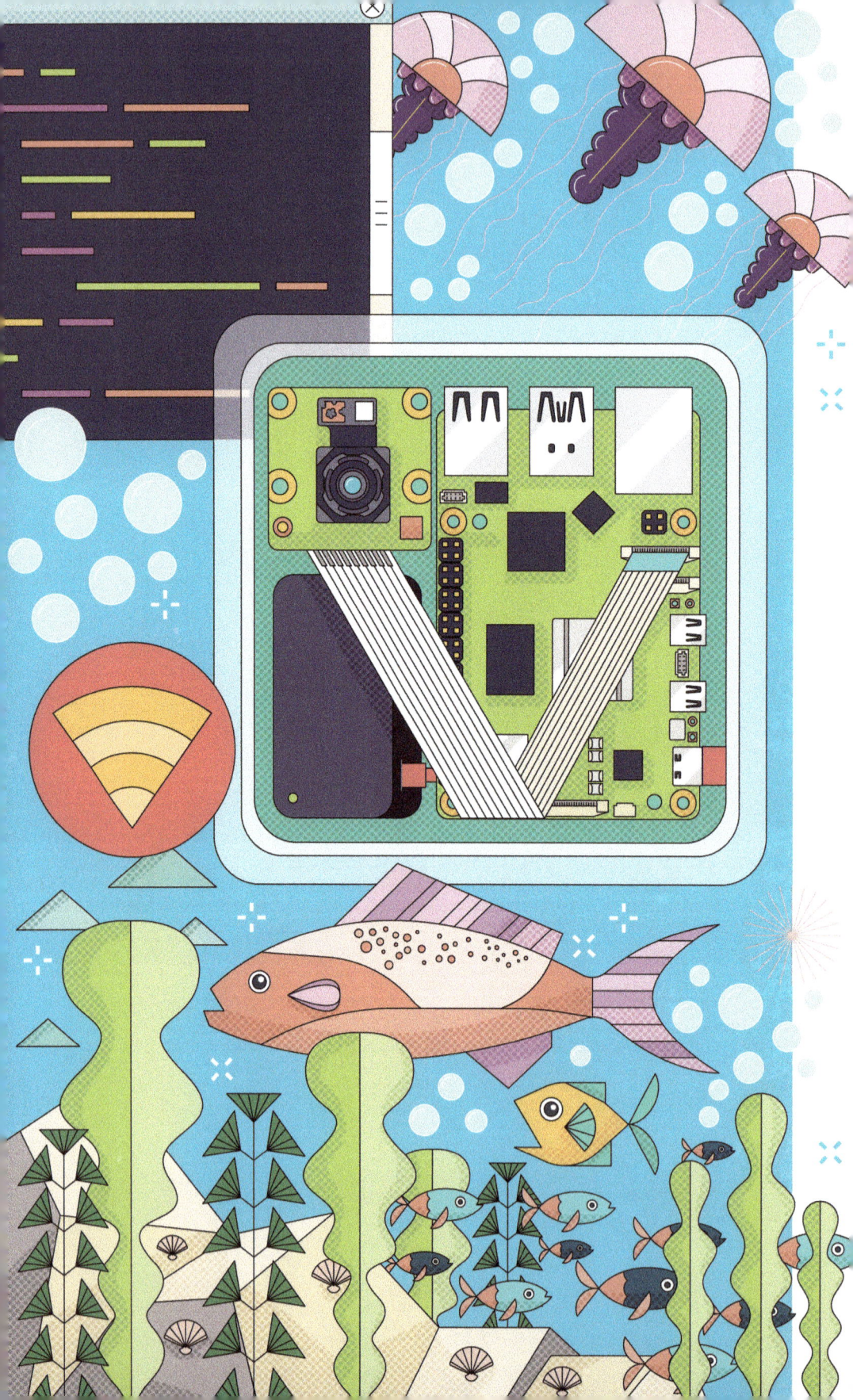

Chapter 16

Take your camera underwater

Explore the underwater world with your camera

There are plenty of underwater sports cameras available, but they can be quite expensive, especially if you want to be able to control them remotely. In this chapter we're going to use readily available Raspberry Pi add-ons to make a cheaper, customisable camera unit. There are lots of options and alternative sources of components for a project like this. For example, the Pimoroni Enviro board (or earlier Enviro pHAT) can report back information about the environment in which the camera is operating, especially how much light is available.

You'll need

- Camera Module / HQ Camera
- Transparent, waterproof box (**magpi.cc/waterproofcase**)
- Ethernet cable
- Waterproof putty or epoxy
- Portable power source
- Enviro board (optional: **magpi.cc/enviro**)
- ZeroView (optional: **magpi.cc/zeroview**)

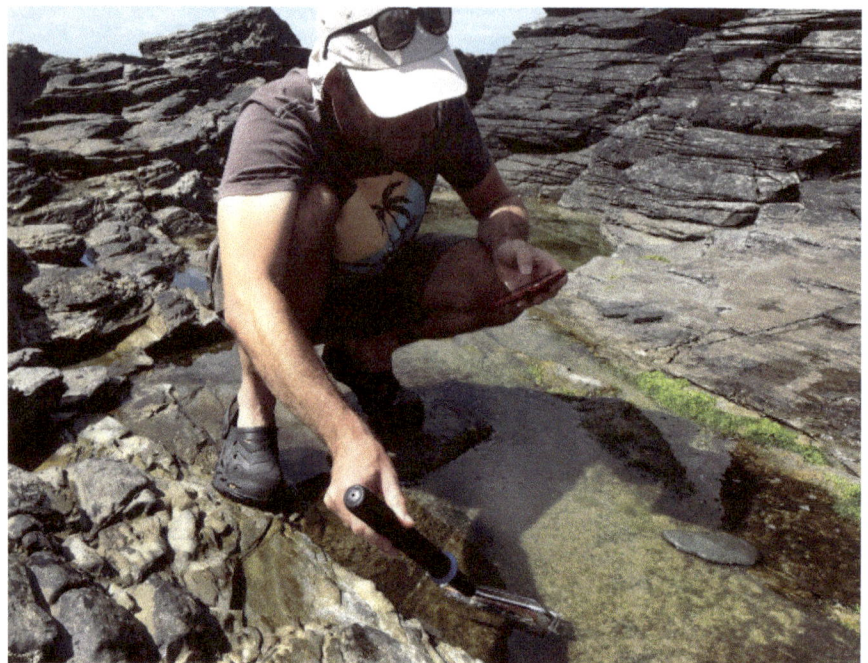

Figure 16-1 You'll still have to get pretty close to the water yourself

Find a suitable container

To protect the electronics inside it, the container for your Raspberry Pi and camera needs to be watertight and to have at least a see-through lid. You can find food container boxes with a very tight seal, but these tend to be translucent rather than transparent. The size of box will probably determine your choice of Raspberry Pi model and power source, though you should choose a model with Ethernet. You can save space by using a LiPo battery instead of a standard power bank (although you'll need a boost regulator too, such as the Pimoroni LiPo SHIM, shown in **Figure 16-2**).

Configure your Raspberry Pi

Start from a fresh Raspberry Pi OS install on a microSD card. Open up a Terminal window and enter the following commands to update the APT database and install the required packages:

```
sudo apt update
sudo apt install -y python3-flask
```

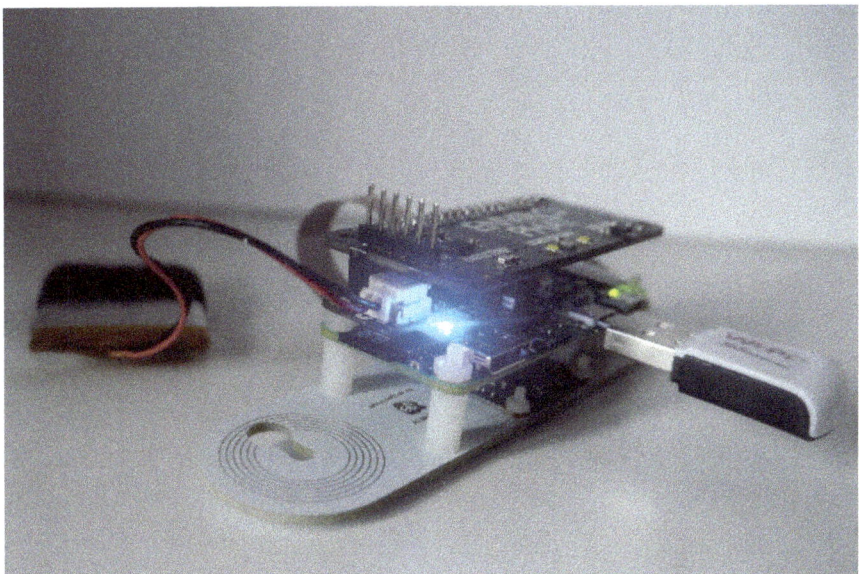

Figure 16-2 You can save space by using a LiPo battery (via a boost regulator) instead of a power bank

Radio signals, including WiFi, do not propagate underwater at all well. Because of this, we recommend you use an Ethernet cable to connect to your Raspberry Pi in the field. You'll need to drill a hole in your container to pass in the Ethernet cable and then seal the hole with waterproof putty or epoxy. If you can find an Ethernet cable that is rated for underwater use, it will last longer and won't endanger any of your electronics.

Add some code, HTML and CSS

Flask is a tiny web application framework for Python. It lets you build web applications without a lot of fuss. There are two parts to the Flask application you'll use in this chapter: the main program, and the *template*. Let's start with the main program.

Create a subdirectory named **Flask** in your home directory (`mkdir ~/Flask`). Then, in the Thonny code editor, create a file with the following code, and save it in the **Flask** directory as **camera_underwater.py**. You can also create this file in any text editor or download it from the book's GitHub repository (see *Welcome* on page v for details on downloading sample code).

```python
from flask import Flask, render_template,request, redirect, url_for
import os, shutil
from picamera2 import Picamera2
from datetime import datetime
from subprocess import call

app = Flask(__name__)
app.config['SEND_FILE_MAX_AGE_DEFAULT'] = 1

# Make the a subdirectory for images.
os.makedirs("static", exist_ok = True)

started = False # Make sure we only create the camera object once!
def start_camera():
    global started, cam, message
    if not started:
        cam = Picamera2()
        message = "Camera ready"
        started = True

def take_picture(): # take a picture

    global message

    t='{:%Y%m%d-%H%M%S}'.format(datetime.now())
    filename = 'snap'+t+'.jpg'
    # Take the photo
    cam.start_and_capture_file(f"static/{filename}",
                                show_preview=False)
    # Copy it to the latest.jpg file
    shutil.copyfile(f"static/{filename}", 'static/latest.jpg')

    message = f"Took photo: {filename}"

@app.route('/', methods = ['POST','GET'])
def hello_world():

    global message

    start_camera() # Start up the camera

    if request.method == 'POST':

        if request.form['submit'] == 'Take Photo':
            take_picture()
        elif request.form['submit'] == 'Shutdown':
```

```
            call("sudo shutdown --poweroff now", shell=True)
        else:
            pass

    df = os.statvfs('/') # are we running out of disk space?
    df_size = df.f_frsize * df.f_blocks
    df_avail = df.f_frsize * df.f_bfree
    df_pc = round(100 -(100 * df_avail/df_size),1)

    # Display the web page template with our template variables
    return render_template('index.html', message=message,
                            df_pc=df_pc)

if __name__ == "__main__":

    # let's launch our site!
    app.run(host='0.0.0.0',port=5000,debug=True)
```

The main program (**camera_underwater.py**) drives everything, taking pictures, copying files, shutting down your Raspberry Pi. The main program also takes care of rendering the web page by loading the template.

Everything starts running with the one line of code at the end of the file. The **hello_world()** function that appears before it is the main function of the program. Flask knows to run it when someone loads the root page of the website (**/**) thanks to the *decorator* that precedes the function definition (**@app.route('/', methods = ['POST','GET'])**).

Next, create one subdirectory named **static** (to hold images) and one named **templates** under the **Flask** directory:

```
mkdir ~/Flask/static
mkdir ~/Flask/templates
```

Create the following file in your favourite text editor and save it in **~/Flask/templates** as **index.html**. This will be the main HTML file for your application. The variables between **{** and **}** in the code are replaced with their values when your Python program serves up the web page:

```
<!DOCTYPE html>
<html>
<head>
        <meta charset="utf-8">
        <title>AquaPiCam</title>
        <style>
```

```html
        .button {
            display: inline-block;
            font-size: 24px;
            text-align: center;
            color: #fff;
            background-color: #4CAF50;
        }
        .button:hover { background-color: #3e8e41 }
        .center { text-align: center; }
        body {
            font: 100 1.5em Helvetica, Arial, sans-serif;
            background-color: grey;
        }
        h1 { color: #0000ff; }
        h2 { color: #6600cc; }
        h3 { color: #003300; }
        </style>
</head>
<body>
    <h1 class="center">AquaPiCam!</h1>
    <h2 class="center">Free disk space: {{ df_pc }}%</h2>
    <h3 class="center">Message: {{ message }} </h3>
    <form class="center" action="/" method="post">
        <input class="button" type="submit"
                name="submit" value="Take Photo">
        <input class="button" type="submit"
           onclick="return confirm('Really shut down?');"
                name="submit" value="Shutdown">
    </form>
    <div class="center"><p>Latest image:</p>
        <img src="../static/latest.jpg" width="480" height="287"
            alt="Last"/>
    </div>
</body>
</html>
```

The HTML file defines two buttons: one to take a picture (**Take Photo**) and another to shut down your Raspberry Pi (**Shutdown**). This will allow you to safely shut down even if you don't have a keyboard and mouse attached.

Open a Terminal, **cd** to the **Flask** directory and run the program:

```
cd ~/Flask
python3 camera_underwater.py
```

To see the generated web page from another computer or mobile device, make sure you're connected to the same network as your Raspberry Pi, open a web browser, and enter **http://hostname:5000**. Replace **hostname** with your Raspberry Pi's hostname (if you have trouble connecting with the hostname, try replacing it with the Raspberry Pi's IP address).

You'll be greeted by the web page shown in **Figure 16-3**. You have two options: take a picture and shutdown the Raspberry Pi. Take all the pictures you want, and when you're done, click the Shutdown button and then click OK to shut it down.

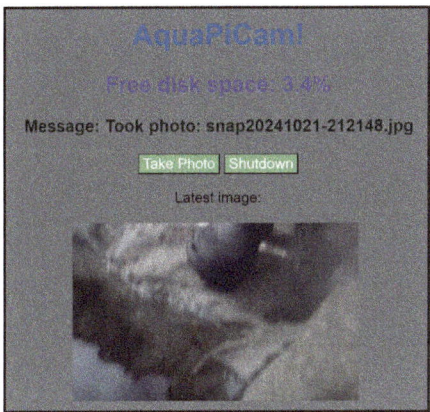

Figure 16-3 The web interface shows environmental information and lets you control the camera

Set the code to run at boot

Naturally, you'll want the code to run automatically whenever the Raspberry Pi boots up. To do so, open up a Terminal window and edit your *cron table* with **crontab -e**. You may be asked to select an editor the first time you run this command. When the editor appears, go to the bottom of the file, and add this line, then save the file and exit the editor:

@reboot (cd Flask; /usr/bin/python camera_underwater.py)

This will ensure that the script runs under your user credentials each time the system boots.

In addition, to get Raspberry Pi to boot up slightly faster and to use a little less power so your battery lasts longer, it's best to get it to boot directly to the command line rather than booting to the desktop. See "Boot your Pi to the CLI" on page 110 for details.

To stop the script while it's running, you can run the following command. Unlike **pidof**, which only searches the name of the executable, **pgrep -f** searches a process' command-line arguments, including the script name:

```
kill $(pgrep -f camera_underwater.py)
```

Now go and find somewhere wet! You might want to run a few tests in the bath before venturing further afield.

Fitting everything into your container

To cut down on reflections and obtain the best possible images, the camera should be as close to the transparent side of your container as possible. The ZeroView from the Pi Hut is a clever mounting plate that uses suction cups and will also hold your Raspberry Pi Zero securely. Alternatively, you could make a mount out of cardboard and glue this to the inside of the container. Velcro tape can be a good solution for power sources (which normally need to be removable for recharging). **Figure 16-4** shows our version of the project, ready to be immersed!

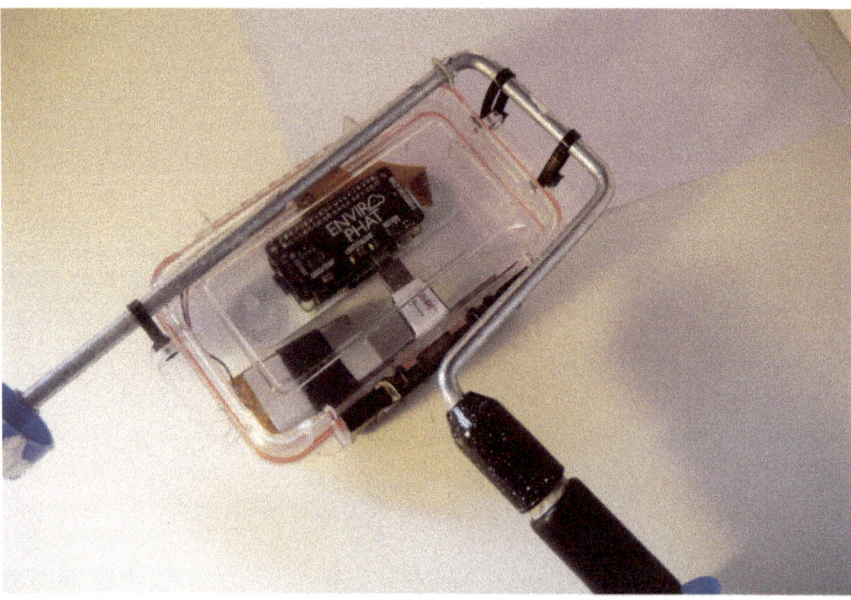

Figure 16-4 A makeshift handle to lower the waterproof box into the water

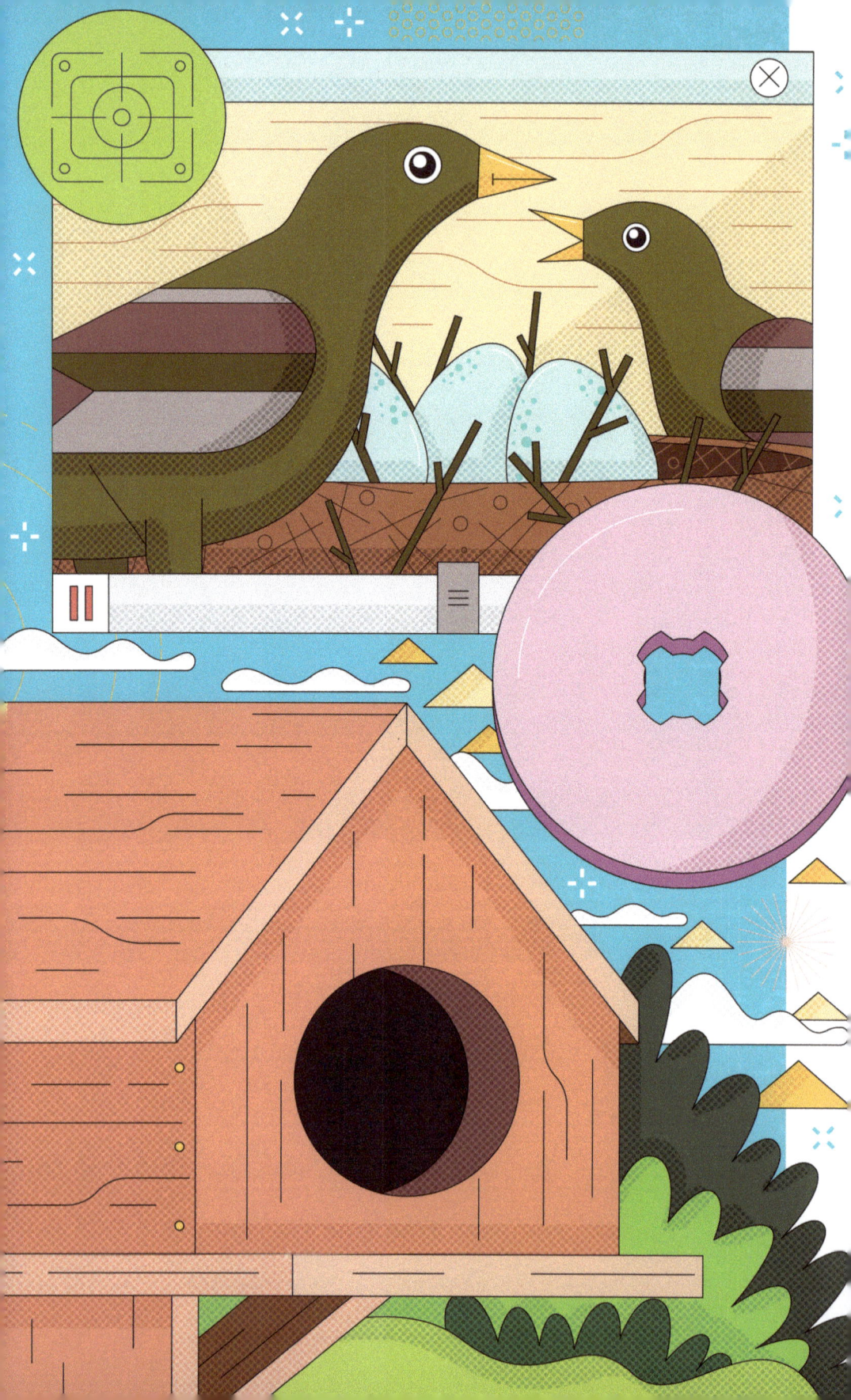

Chapter 17

Install a bird box camera

Observe nesting birds without disturbing them

While it's simple enough to set up a Camera Module in a weatherproof box to observe wildlife in your garden, for this project we'll be installing a camera inside a bird box. Since it'll be dark inside, and we can't use a standard light source, we'll need to use a Pi NoIR Camera Module. 'NoIR' stands for 'no infrared', as it omits the IR filter found in the standard camera. This enables you to use an infrared light source to see in the dark. Note that we'll need to adjust the fixed focus of the camera by unscrewing the lens.

You'll need

- Pi NoIR Camera Module
- Focus adjustment tool
- Bird box
- IR LED
- Female-to-female jumper wires
- Power source
- Ethernet cable (optional)

Prepare your camera

We can't use a standard light source inside the bird box, since this could attract insects and predators, and so would deter any birds from nesting there. So we need to use a Pi NoIR Camera Module (see **Figure 17-1**). Apart from the omission of an infrared filter, this works exactly the same way as the standard camera, so you can connect it up to your Raspberry Pi as in Chapter 1 and use all the same Terminal commands. So, for instance, you can obtain a video preview with:

`rpicam-vid -t 0`

You'll notice that everything looks a little strange; this is because you're looking at a combination of visible light and infrared light. To test it out in darkness, turn the lights off, aim a TV remote control at your face and press the buttons to produce an IR light source. You should see your face illuminated in the darkness. The image will look black and white (greyscale), because there are no wavelengths of light from the visible spectrum being detected. However, a black and white image is good enough to allow you to watch what's happening inside a bird box, and it doesn't disturb or interfere with the birds in any way. Press **CTRL+C** to exit the preview.

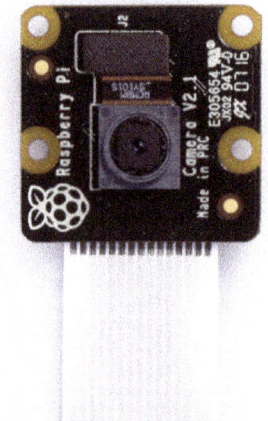

Figure 17-1 The Pi NoIR Camera Module can see in the dark with infrared lighting

> **? HQ Camera**
>
> If you want to use an HQ Camera for this project, you'll need to remove its IR filter so it can capture infrared images in the dark. See the leaflet supplied with the camera for more details but note that this is an irreversible process.

Wire up an IR LED

We'll need a suitable infrared light source in the bird box. In this example we're using a single IR LED, but alternatives include small IR lamps and the IR version of the LISIPAROI (**lisiparoi.com**). Our 890 nm IR LED is an identical component to the ones found inside TV remote controls; the only difference is that we're going to keep it on constantly when shooting video or stills in the bird box.

As usual, you should turn off your Raspberry Pi before connecting anything up. If you've wired up an LED to Raspberry Pi's GPIO pins before, then please note that this LED needs to be done slightly differently. Since an infrared LED requires more current than the GPIO pins can provide, it needs to be connected directly to the 5V supply of Raspberry Pi with a 220Ω resistor inline; without the resistor the current will be too high, and the LED will burn out after about ten seconds.

Figure 17-2 shows how the LED should be wired up. You'll notice that the LED has two legs, one slightly longer than the other. The longer of the two is called the anode and the shorter is the cathode. The LED needs power to flow into the anode and out of the cathode; if you get the polarity wrong then nothing will happen.

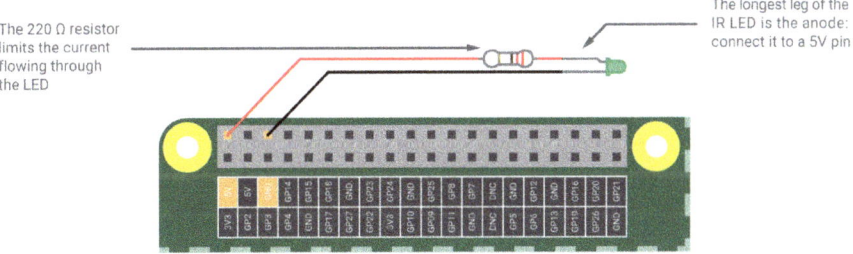

Figure 17-2 Wiring up the birdbox

Use a couple of female-to-female jumper wires to make the following connections. Connect the anode (long leg) to 5 V, which is the first pin on the outside row on the GPIO. Connect the cathode (short leg) to the 220Ω resistor. Connect the other side of the resistor to ground (GND), which is the third pin in on the outside row of the GPIO.

Test the LED

With everything wired up correctly, turn your Raspberry Pi back on. You'll notice that the infrared LED doesn't appear to be working, but in fact it is. Your human eyes can't see it, but the Pi NoIR camera can. Turn on the camera preview again with **rpicam-vid -t 0**. Hold the LED in front of the camera and you should see it lit. If not, then you may have mixed up the polarity of the anode and cathode. Double-check your wiring against the Figure 2 diagram. Try turning out the lights and aiming the LED at yourself; don't look directly into it, however, as infrared light can still cause harm to your eyes. You'll see from the Pi NoIR camera preview that it will illuminate you quite well. Press **CTRL+C** when you want to exit.

Install the camera

Place your finger on the roof, approximately above the centre of the main body of the bird box. Lift up the roof and place your thumb directly below your finger, so that you're pinching the lid as shown in **Figure 17-3**. Your thumb is now where the camera needs to be. Take a pen and mark this spot with a cross. Cut out a rectangle of cardboard approximately 4 cm × 2 cm (1.5" × 0.75") and fold it in half lengthways. Use some tape to secure it to the underside of the roof so that it's a few millimetres below the cross. This is going to be used to compensate for the angle of the roof, so that the camera points directly into the middle of the bird box.

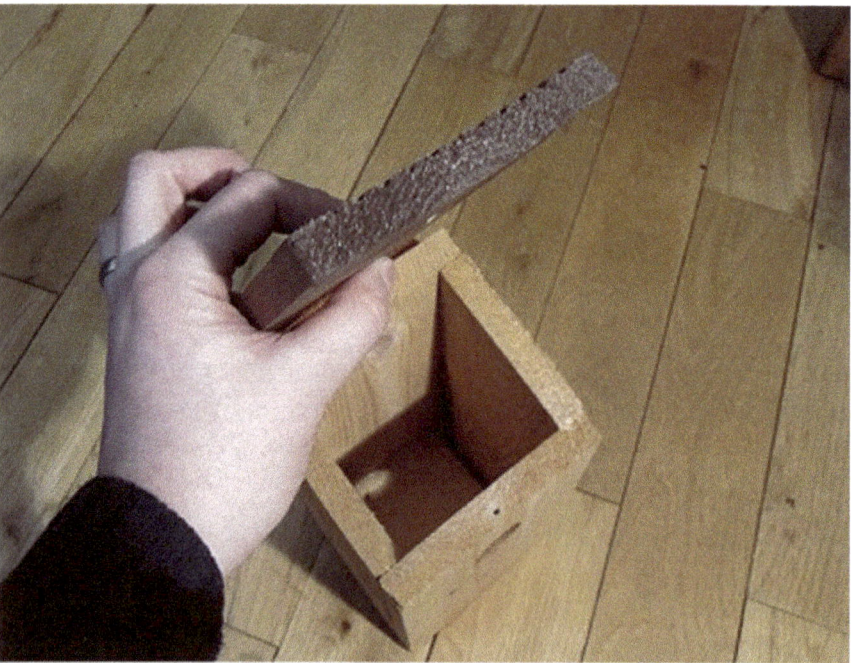

Figure 17-3   Pinch the lid and then use a pen to mark a cross where your thumb is

Next, take the Pi NoIR and slide the flexible cable down between the roof hinge and the back wall of the box (see **Figure 17-4**). Do this with the tin connectors facing away from the back wall. If you wish, you can remove the two middle staples holding the hinge in place; this will make the flex exit the bird box more neatly.

Take some tape and put it across the top of the Pi NoIR board — do not cover the camera lens! Secure the camera in place so that the central lens is directly over the cross that you drew earlier. The camera should sit at an angle as shown in **Figure 17-5**. Close the lid and inspect the camera angle from the side: it needs to point directly at the centre of the base. If it doesn't look right, then go back and adjust it until you're happy. An alternative to taping it in place would be to use the four mounting holes to screw it to the lid via a wedge of wood instead of the cardboard.

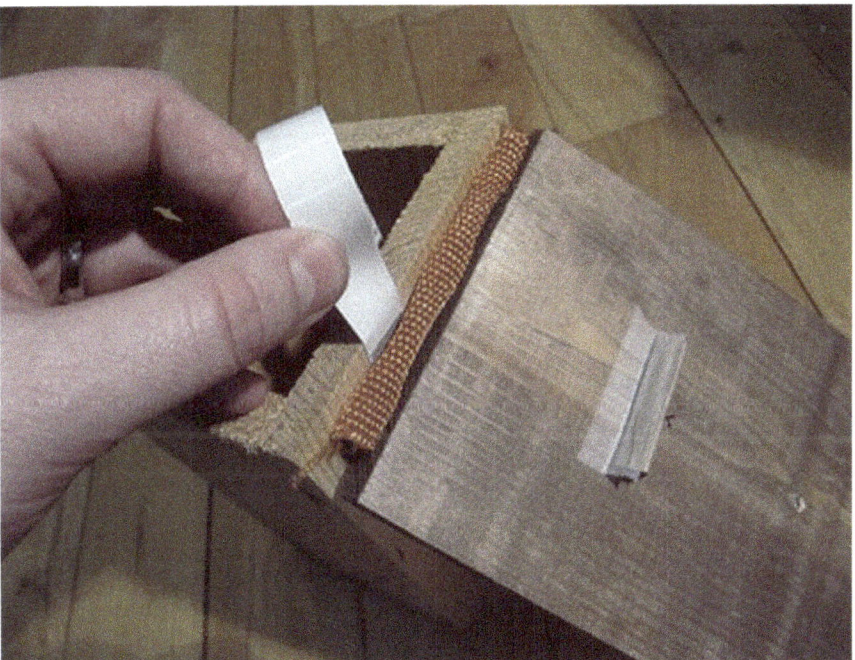

Figure 17-4 Slide the camera cable between the roof hinge and the back wall of the box

Add the LED

Secure the infrared LED to the underside of the roof. Don't attach it too close to the camera, or you'll see a lot of glare on the video. The LED can go anywhere, but it can help to bend its legs by 90 degrees and secure it to the roof that way (see **Figure 17-6**). You may also wish to blank off the end of the LED

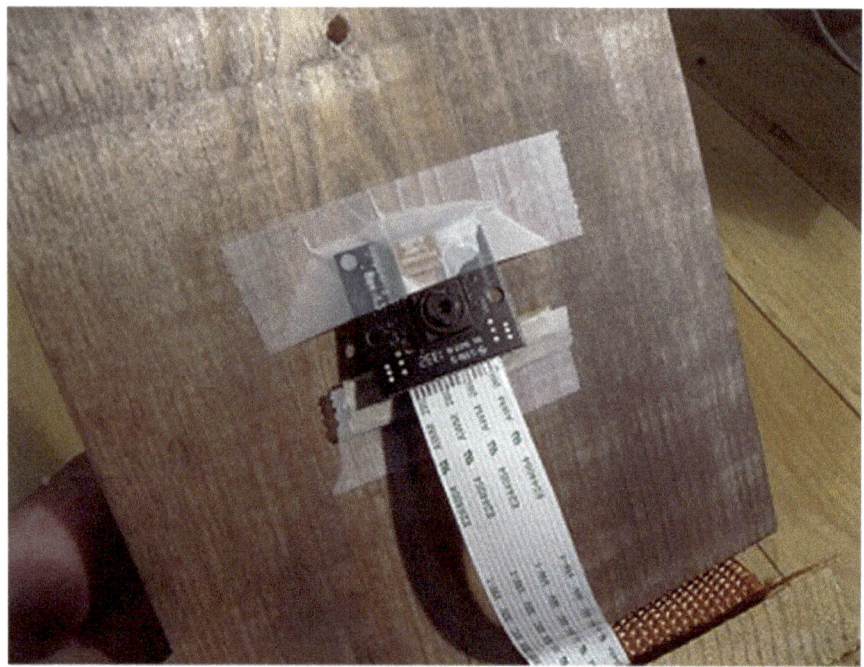

Figure 17-5 When in place, the camera should sit at an angle to compensate for the roof slope

with correction fluid or by filing it down with a nail file. This will prevent any spotlight effect on the video and give a more diffuse light.

Test it again

Now reconnect your Raspberry Pi and test the focus once again. We recommend connecting the camera flex coming from the back of the bird box to Raspberry Pi first. Then connect the LED and resistor, followed by the screen, keyboard, and finally the power supply. When testing this setup, it can be helpful to rest Raspberry Pi upside-down on the roof of the bird box, but do whatever works best for you.

Boot up as usual and then start the video preview with `rpicam-vid -t 0`. With the roof of the bird box closed, you should be able to see the inside in black and white. This shows that the infrared illumination is working; you should even be able to cover the hole and still see the inside. It will look similar to the image shown in **Figure 17-7**, but will be slightly more zoomed in. This is because this image was taken using the `rpicam-still` command and not `rpicam-vid`. If you can't see anything at all, then it's likely the LED is not

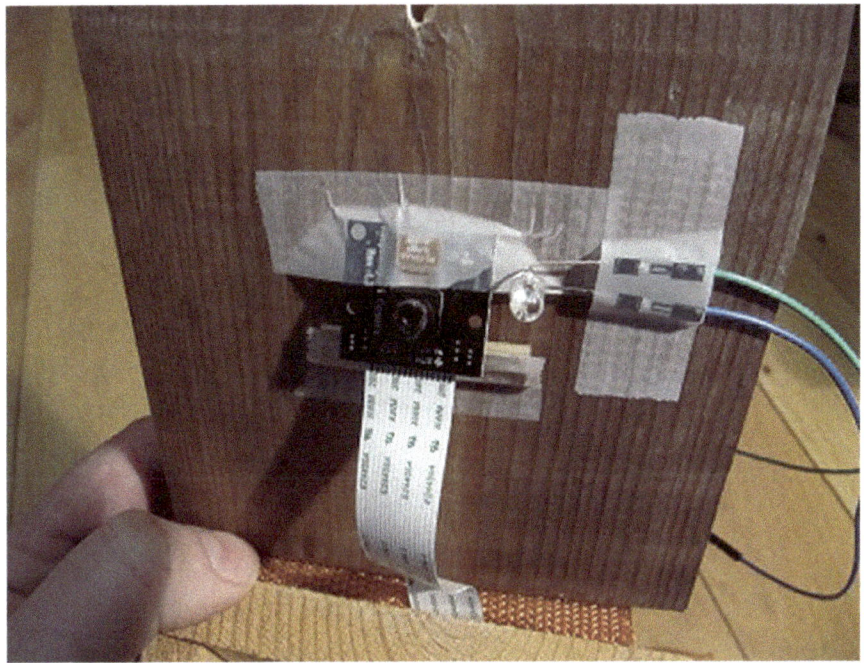

Figure 17-6   The IR LED is taped to the underside of the roof, not too close to the camera

wired up correctly: double-check the wiring and the polarity of the anode and cathode.

It's now helpful to put an object with some black-on-white text into the bird box to verify the focus, such as a watch or business card. Ensure that the text is in focus and readable; adjust the camera focus again as necessary before continuing. Remember to compensate for the nest height. Press **CTRL+C** when you want to stop the camera preview.

Weatherproof it

While you can attach your Raspberry Pi directly to the outside of the bird box, an alternative is to use a longer camera cable. Either way, you'll need to put Raspberry Pi inside a weatherproof box. Preventing water getting into the bird box should also be a priority. The roof could be sealed using silicone sealant, which is often used to seal the edges of windows and bathroom sinks. Choosing a site which is beneath the overhang of an existing roof will help a lot, so the bird box will not be rained on directly.

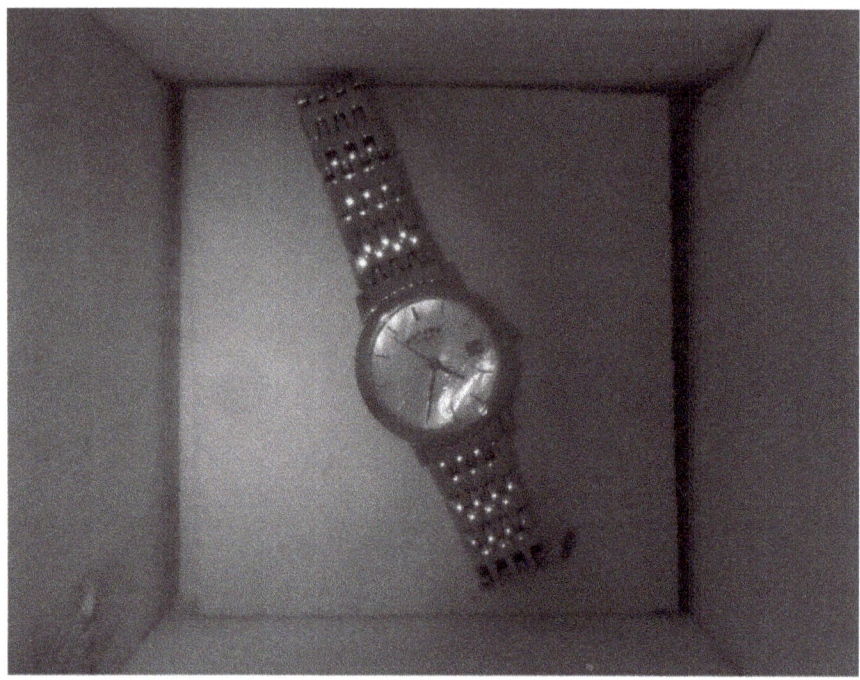

Figure 17-7 Make sure that the test object is raised up slightly and the text is in focus

Lastly, you need to consider how you will get power and an internet connection to the bird box? You could use a wireless USB dongle, or the built-in wireless LAN of a Raspberry Pi 3 / 3B+ / 4 / Zero W, but Ethernet is more reliable for streaming video, especially in built-up areas that have a lot of wireless traffic.

Obtain images

With everything installed, connected, and powered up, you can SSH in to your Raspberry Pi from another computer (see **magpi.cc/ssh** for details) to control it remotely. You are then able to enter standard Terminal commands such as **rpicam-still** and **rpicam-vid** to obtain stills (including time-lapses, described in Chapter 8, *Time-lapse photography*) and video footage. You could also write one or more Python scripts using the PiCamera2 library.

If you'd like to capture true black and white images, you can do this by taking down the colour saturation completely. Just add the **--saturation 0** argument to **rpicam-still** and **rpicam-vid** to remove all colour from the resulting image.

Note that you can't view the live camera preview via SSH. However, you can live-stream video from the bird box. This could be achieved using a client-server setup, to pipe the output to a video player on the client computer. Alternatively, you could make use of an internet video service offering live streaming, such as YouTube (see **magpi.cc/birdboxyt** for details).

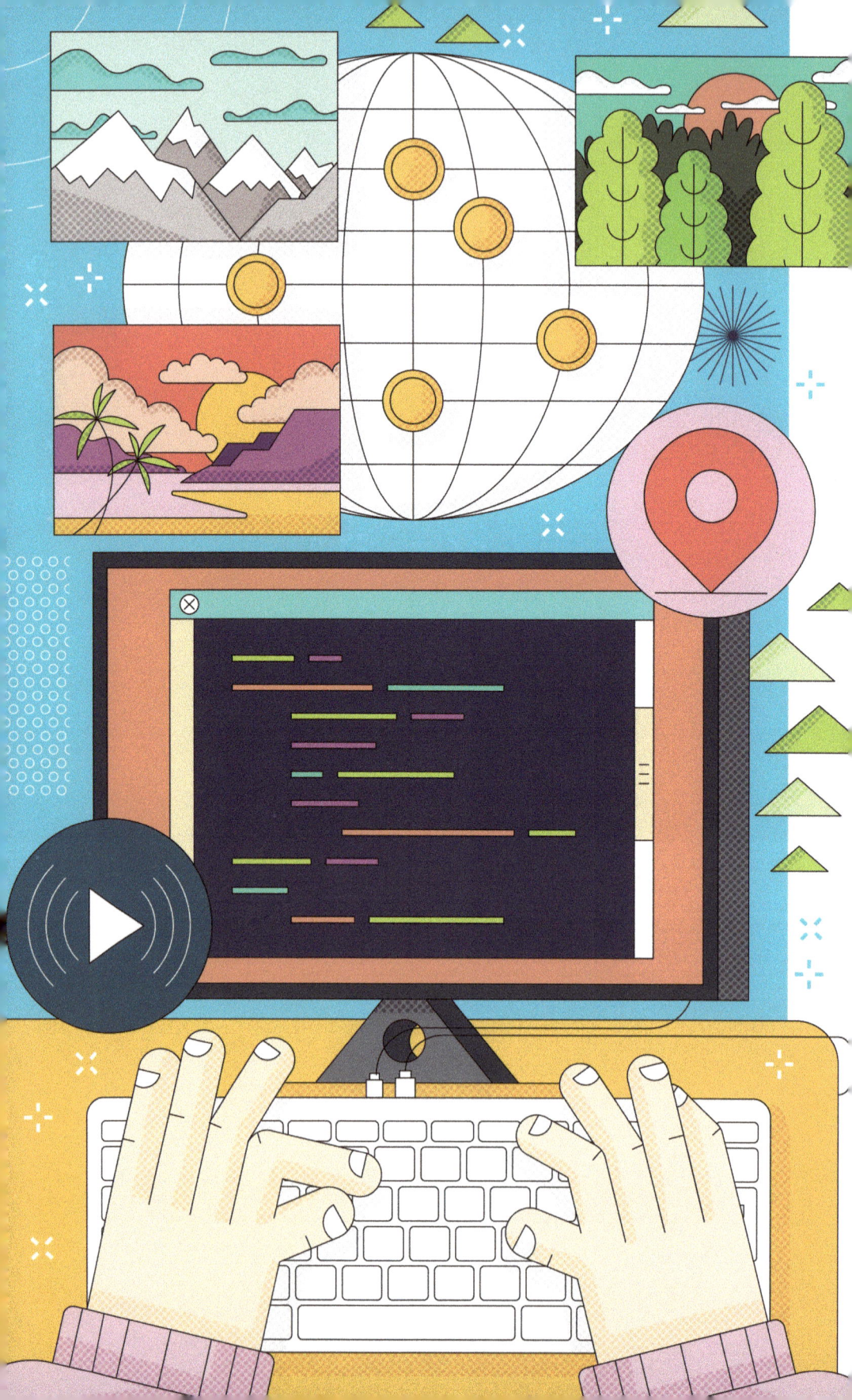

Chapter 18

Live-stream video and stills

Stream video and regular stills to a remote computer

One of the drawbacks of using SSH or VNC to access your Camera Module- or HQ Camera-equipped Raspberry Pi remotely from another computer is that you can't (typically) view the camera preview via these methods. To get around this, you'll need to stream live video across the network. While there are various methods available for doing this, in this chapter we'll show you how to create a client-server setup for video streaming using the picamera2 Python library. We'll also explore how to send a stream of stills over the network.

You'll need

- Camera Module / HQ Camera
- Remote computer

Streaming video

In the Thonny code editor, create a new file with the following code, and save it as **stream_video.py** and run it. You can also create this file in any editor or download it from the book's GitHub repository and then run it with **python stream_video.py**.

See *Welcome* on page v for details on downloading sample code.

```python
import socket
import time

from picamera2 import Picamera2
from picamera2.encoders import H264Encoder
from picamera2.outputs import FileOutput

# Configure the camera
cam = Picamera2()
vid_config = cam.create_video_configuration({"size": (1280, 720)})
cam.configure(vid_config)
encoder = H264Encoder(1000000)
cam.encoders = encoder

# Listen on a socket for connections
with socket.socket(socket.AF_INET, socket.SOCK_STREAM) as sock:
    sock.setsockopt(socket.SOL_SOCKET, socket.SO_REUSEADDR, 1)
    sock.bind(("0.0.0.0", 8888))
    sock.listen()

    # Each time through the loop, stream video until the
    # client disconnects.
    try:
        while True:
            conn, addr = sock.accept()
            stream = conn.makefile("wb")
            encoder.output = FileOutput(stream)
            cam.start_encoder(encoder)
            cam.start()

            # Wait until the client disconnects
            try:
                while(conn.recv(512)):
                    pass
            except ConnectionResetError:
                pass

            print("Client disconnected.")
            cam.stop()
            cam.stop_encoder()
            conn.close()
    except KeyboardInterrupt: # Press CTRL+C to quit.
        print("Received CTRL+C, exiting.")
        sock.close()
```

Run the code on your Raspberry Pi, then open VLC on another computer, click **File**, then choose **Open** Network. In the URL field, type **tcp/h264://hostname:8888** and replace **hostname** with your Raspberry Pi's hostname (try its IP address if the hostname doesn't work). You should see the stream appear as shown in **Figure 18-1**. To stop the stream, go back to your Raspberry Pi, and press **CTRL+C** in the Terminal session where it's running.

If you have difficulty viewing the stream from VLC, you can try another player, such as *ffplay*, *mpv*, or *smplayer*. You could also try another approach to streaming video frames — the **mjpeg_server_2.py** example from the PiCamera2 repository lets you stream in the MJPEG format, runs in a browser, and supports multiple simultaneous viewers: **magpi.cc/mjpegserver**.

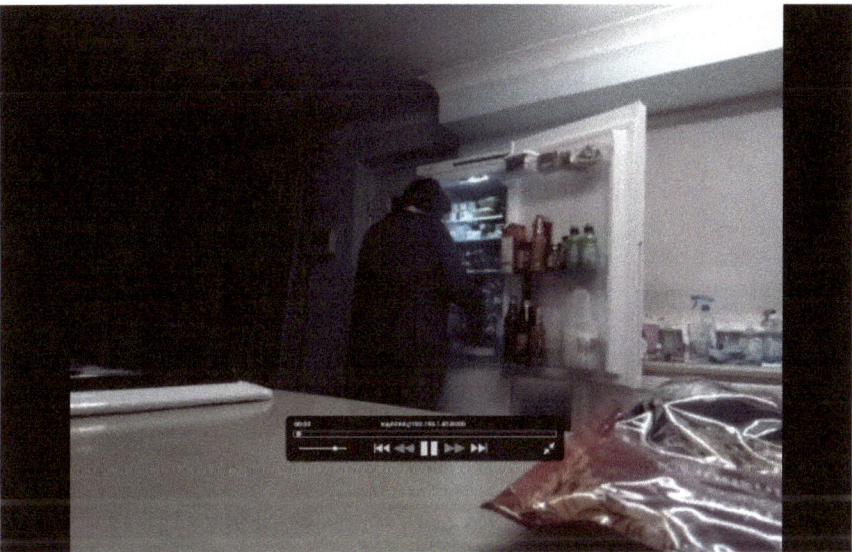

Figure 18-1 Opening the network source in VLC or another media player

Stream stills

Now let's stream camera stills taken at regular intervals in a variation on a standard time-lapse setup. Running on a remote computer (which could be another Raspberry Pi), the server script, **receive_images.py**, starts a socket to listen for a connection from your Raspberry Pi with the camera.

```
import io
import os
import socket
import struct
```

```python
from time import sleep
from PIL import Image
from datetime import datetime

# Start a socket listening for connections on
# 0.0.0.0:8000 (0.0.0.0 means all interfaces)
server_socket = socket.socket()
server_socket.bind(('0.0.0.0', 8088))
server_socket.listen(0)

folder = "pictures"
os.makedirs(folder, exist_ok = True) # A folder to store images.

print("Ready for connections.")
try:
    while True:
        # Accept a connection and make a file-like object for it.
        conn, addr = server_socket.accept()
        stream = conn.makefile('rb')
        try:
            while True:
                # Read the image length as a 32-bit unsigned int.
                # If the length is zero, quit the loop.
                length = stream.read(struct.calcsize('<L'))
                image_len = struct.unpack('<L', length)[0]
                print(image_len)
                if not image_len:
                    break
                # Construct a stream to hold the image data and
                # read the image data from the connection.
                image_stream = io.BytesIO()
                image_stream.write(stream.read(image_len))
                # Rewind the stream, open it as an image with PIL
                # and save it in the image folder
                image_stream.seek(0)
                image = Image.open(image_stream)
                ts = str(datetime.now()) # get a timestamp
                image.save(os.path.join(folder, ts) + ".jpg")

        finally:
            conn.close()
except KeyboardInterrupt: # Press CTRL+C to quit.
    print("Received CTRL+C, exiting.")
    server_socket.close()
```

At the top, we import the required libraries; here we're using PIL (you can install it using **pip install pillow**) to read JPEG files (see "Object detection with YOLO" on page 124 for an example of setting up a virtual environment for installing your own packages). The script then checks the image length and, if it is not zero, constructs a stream to hold the image data and then reads it from the connection. The **image.save()** command will save each image in the **pictures** subdirectory: it can create a lot of windows if left going for a while! Now to create a client script...

Stills client script

On your Raspberry Pi with the camera, the client script, **send_images.py**, sends a continual stream of images to the server.

```
import io
import socket
import struct
import time
from picamera2 import Picamera2

# Connect a client socket to my_server:8088 (change my_server to
# the hostname of your server)
client_socket = socket.socket()
client_socket.connect(('my_server', 8088))

# Make a file-like object out of the connection
connection = client_socket.makefile('wb')
try:
    cam = Picamera2()
    # Start a preview and let the camera warm up for 2 seconds
    cam.start()
    time.sleep(2)

    # Construct a stream to hold image data temporarily (we could
    # write it directly to connection but in this case we want the
    # size of each image first to keep our protocol simple).
    stream = io.BytesIO()
    for i in range(0, 15): # Capture 15 images
        stream = io.BytesIO()
        cam.capture_file(stream, format='jpeg')

        # Write the length of the capture to the stream and flush
        # to ensure it actually gets sent
        connection.write(struct.pack('<L', stream.tell()))
        connection.flush()
```

```python
    # Rewind the stream and send the image data over the wire
    stream.seek(0)
    connection.write(stream.read())

    # Pause
    time.sleep(2)

    # Reset the stream for the next capture
    stream.seek(0)
    stream.truncate()

    # Write a length of zero to the stream to signal we're done
    connection.write(struct.pack('<L', 0))
finally:
    connection.close()
    client_socket.close()
```

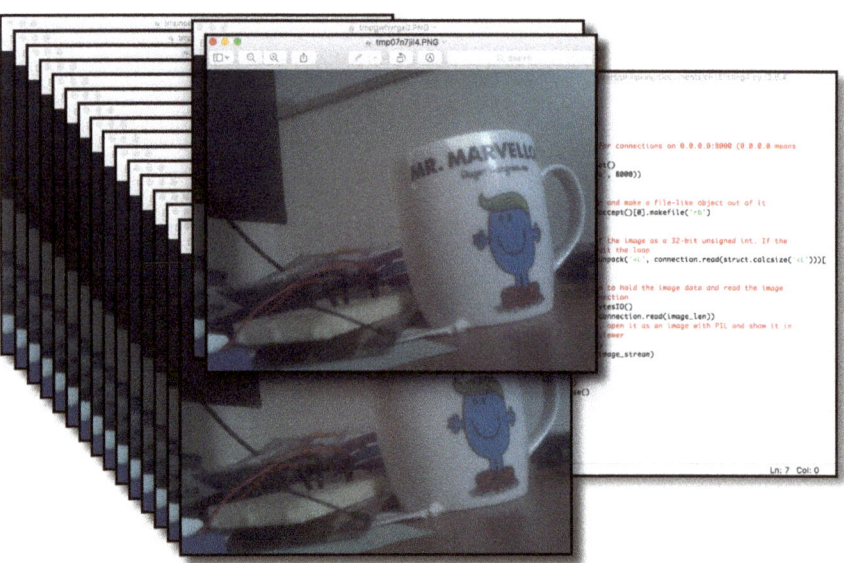

Figure 18-2 Multiple stills are streamed to the remote computer and displayed

We use a very simple protocol for communication: first, the length of the image will be sent as a 32-bit integer (in little-endian format), then this will be followed by the bytes of image data. If the length is 0, this indicates that the connection should be closed as no more images will be forthcoming. As before, for connecting the socket, you should replace **my_server** in the script with the host name of the remote computer. We then make a file-like object out of the connection. Before constructing the stream, we start a preview to let the camera warm up for two seconds. Further down, the line `for i in range(0, 15):` limits the number of images to 15, though you can alter this.

You could replace `image.save(os.path.join(folder, ts) + ".jpg")` in receive_images.py with `image.show()`, and it will display one window for every image captured. **Figure 18-2** shows how this would look.

Note that you should run the server script first to ensure there's a listening socket ready to accept a connection from the client script. Taking it further, rather than simply showing the images, you could use the numerous functions of PIL to process them (see **effbot.org/imagingbook**).

www.ingramcontent.com/pod-product-compliance
Lightning Source LLC
Chambersburg PA
CBHW040521220526
45473CB00013B/2936